A Gift of A Curse:

A Story of Transformation and Triumph

By

Charity Dunson

Table of Contents

Dedication

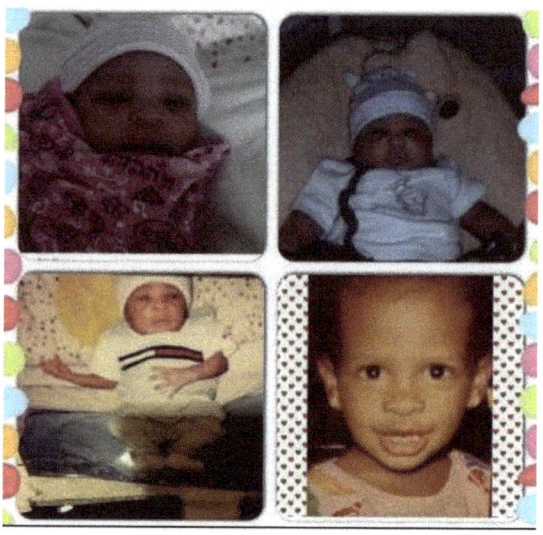

I just wanna take out this time to say Thank You . Yes, you!! You, reading this right now . This book is dedicated to you. I hope and pray you find the strength, the will power and the courage to push through whatever u may be going through right now !! I pray that this book touches your heart in ways you have never experienced. I hope you know you are important and you matter . I wrote this book for you ! I believe that you are created to become whoever you want to be. If you just believe in yourself and know that God is able

1

to help you thru life, Trust me! You can do it . Never give up on your dream … if I did it!! You can do it too ! Start Dreaming ….

I wanna dedicate this book to my three beautiful children because without y'all I don't think there will be no me. Yall give me purpose and a reason to live. I hope this book gives you all peace and understanding . I hope you know how much I love you all and would do anything for you !! This is a part of me that I leave with you forever and ever. I hope I inspire you all to be the best you can be !! You all are talented, beautiful and smart and I love y'all !! I believe in you all to go be the best you can be !!

I would also like to dedicate this book to my mama, my sister, my granny and all my family members who encouraged me . To My therapist , my life coach, mentors, communities, and Morning Miracles w Charity and everyone who inspired me to go harder. WHO believed in me when there was no hope. WHO loved me inspite of my flaws. Y'all the real MVP's.

To my hero - Thank You for believing me ! I love you.

To all my friends, family, and supporters, -

Thank You all too !!

Rest In Heaven 2 The Queen "2024"

Let's Roll –

Chapter 1: Are You, My Mother?

Psalms 27:10 When my father and mother forsake me, then the Lord will take me up.

I was a pretty Baby 🙈

Thoughts to myself echoed such as, why me? Why did I have to be so different? Why was this happening to me? Why couldn't I just be normal? This is what I constantly asked myself. I was born in a cold world with very little understanding and little to no answers. On April 12, 1986, I was born to

Carrie & Marcus. Carrie went into labor around 5:46 am in the hospital with her adopted mama, Mary, and college friends. Carrie pushed out a beautiful baby girl and named her Charity. Funny how she felt so comfortable telling me as I got older that she named me "Charity" because I was a "charity" case. Yet little did she know that God had a different plan.

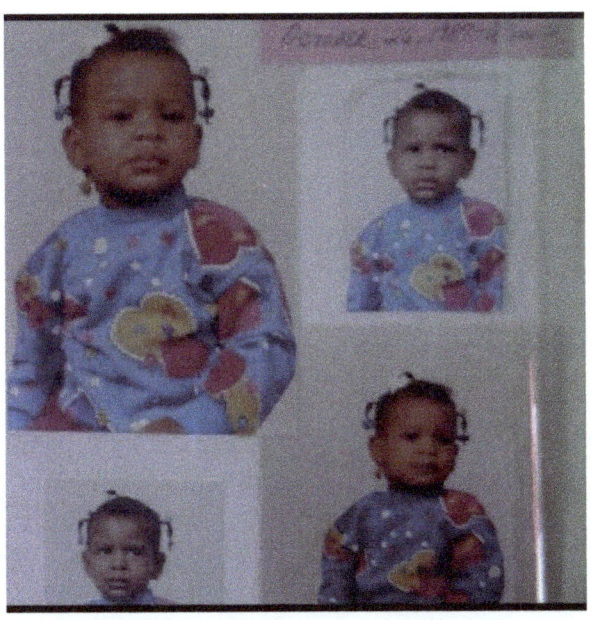

As Mary looked closer at me, she screamed, "OMG!! Carrie! How could you do this? This baby isn't

Mexican! This girl has black ears. Carrie, your father will never accept this. How am I going to explain this?"

When Carrie was born, she was placed in an orphanage in America .She never met her birth parents, and she was later adopted from foster care. Carrie was Italian, German, and Serbian, so I heard. She was adopted by a white couple who were racist. Her now newfound parents hated black people. Carrie had told her mom that she was pregnant with a Mexican baby so they wouldn't upset her father.

Carrie grew up in a small, rich suburb outside of Chicago. Carrie attended Proviso West High School, where she met my dad, Marcus. Marcus was a black man. Marcus's mother had him at the young age of 15. Marcus's mother, my granny, was never raised by her mother. Granny's mother was a big-time drug dealer, and we called her the Queen. Granny was raised by her granny, Big Mama. Seems like I was born into a generational curse.

When Carrie couldn't bring me home, she was put in an uncomfortable situation. With no help from my father, Carrie decided to give me up for adoption. Carrie grew up privileged, knowing very little about public assistance, so she says. I guess she didn't put much effort into finding out, either. So here's where the stories began. This might sound unbelievable, but it's all true, or at least to the best of my knowledge. I might not get every detail right when it comes to when I was a baby, but here we go.

I heard so much growing up that I didn't know what to believe. I grew up very confused and never had any fundamental understanding of anything. As I tell you about my life, I'm sure you'll be confused too. The stories are told about how I went from house to house. I was passed around from person to person. "Nobody wanted me." My now adopted big sister Darla said. I bet nobody ever knew how that made me feel to know nobody wanted me. I heard I stayed in trap houses where drugs were being sold, and they would hide packs in my pamper. I was always crying, and I could see why.

I heard I was sent to Arizona with some rich white people. My grandma the Queen said she gave Carrie "six crispy one-hundred-dollar bills" to fly back out there and get me and bring me back." Why? I always wondered if nobody even wanted me. The Queen didn't even raise her children; Big Mama and my granny did. My dad finally told me that was a lie at thirty-five years old. Marcus told me I was never in Arizona. They lied to the Queen to get the money so he could get high. He was addicted to heroin. All my life, I have heard this story about being with rich people living in Arizona who had written a sad letter about having to give me back, and now come to find out that was a lie too. Wow! Nothing ever made sense to me. None of it was easy to understand. Nobody told the same story, and everything I ever heard was different from everybody else. My life was never easy. Cursed at birth, I used to think. Nothing was ever clear to me or even normal for the matter. Confused should have been my middle name. Having a child should be a gift. A gift from God, but was the gift a curse?

Finally, I ended up in Big Momma's house, my great-great-grandmother's. Big Mama had a house where everyone would bring their kids and leave them when they didn't want to be bothered with them or when they were busy working. Big Mama had a daughter named Lee, who lived upstairs. Lee had one daughter, and at the time, they were older. When they got me, Lee had to be around fifty-five or something like that. Lee's daughter Darla was around thirty years old at the time of my birth. Darla had no kids, and she was Lee's only child.

Darla always told me how Carrie would bring me over and leave me for days and, most times, weeks with no clothes, no pampers, no milk, or nothing. She would always be the one to buy me the things I need. Darla said Carrie would pop up and try to get me, bring me back, and leave me again. Carrie was thinking that the baby would save the relationship with my dad. Marcus was a pimp at the time and was addicted to drugs. My dad didn't care about me and nobody else. He had four boys older than me; I was the baby and the only girl. Carrie thought they could be a family and he would help her raise me, but that never happened. Once my dad abandoned her, she would abandon me again.

I guess Darla eventually got attached to this pretty baby that nobody seemed to want and demanded that Carrie sign over all parental rights. Besides, she wasn't a good mother then anyway, right? She wasn't even ready to be a mother, and since it was a curse on us that she had been given up and her mother had given up, what else could she do? Carrie didn't like Darla very much. If you asked me, I'd say she feared Darla cause Darla didn't take any shit. So, Carrie agreed to give me to Lee. Lee adopted me at six months old and was now my mother. Something else to confuse me to the core. My great auntie on my dad's side was now my mother-in-law, and my cousin was now my sister.

Could you imagine how confusing life was for me? Everyone had two titles, and I now had two mothers and two daddies who were very old at the time, and my sister, who seemed like my mother and acted like my mother, was now my sister. I have been abandoned, rejected, and not accepted since I was born.

I know you're thinking, well, at least you were still in the family, and your cousin and great-aunt took you in, and that should have been good enough, right? I would say right and wrong! There was a void that nothing and nobody could feel or fix. My cousin even told me at the age of sixteen that nobody owed me anything, and the only reason why they got me was because they were older and needed somebody to get the water, get the remote control, and things like that. So now I'm thinking, damn, they just wanted me as an enslaved person? It was very heartbreaking. I didn't ask to be here. All I could think about growing up was, WHY ME?

Chapter 2: Sarah

All thy children will be taught of the Lord. Great shall be the peace of thy children, I Isaiah 54:13

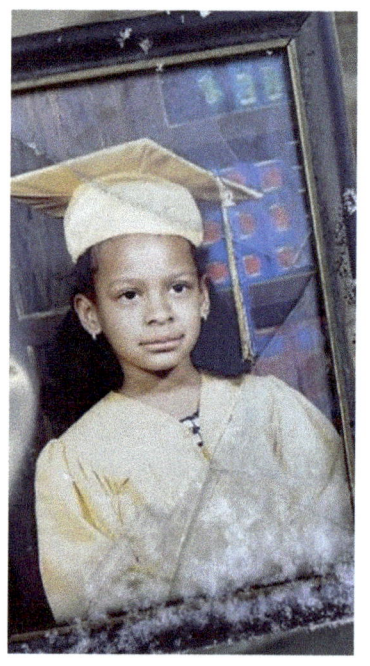

E ven though I was growing up with little to no answers and no understanding, Darla took great care of me. She kept my hair combed, and I always had pretty clothes on. Growing up, I had it all. The big room with a big bed filled with toys, books, and even a computer was significant at that age. Darla and her boyfriend would take me everywhere. I traveled the world and attended everything there was to attend, from ice capades to circuses and zoos. Darla gave me everything a kid could ask for. I'm genuinely grateful to have them in my life.

At the time, Big Mama was alive, and she had a big house that she and her late husband owned before he died. Many lived in this two-flat building on Chicago's westside when Big Mama was alive. She owned a building next door to the courtroom and behind the police station. Many of my girl cousins were teenagers at that time. I was the only baby girl who lived there, and my boy cousin Tune was the baby boy. We were the only two who lived there, but we had other boy cousins who came over a lot and were three to four years older than us. I was one year older than Tune. Tune's mother was on drugs, and she left him there with Big Mama, and he never knew his dad. The house had three bedrooms on the first floor & four bedrooms on the second floor, and one big basement. Big Mama was beautiful. She had long yellow like and grey hair mixed. She had pretty eyes and she wore glasses. She wasn't too big and wasn't too small. Big mama was around 5 feet and 6 inches tall .

Big Mama called me Sarah because she didn't like my name or couldn't say it. Big Mama always cooked meals that I wouldn't say I liked most of the time. She was around eighty-three years old. Big Mama would have these shoestrings tied up together full of keys, and when we got in trouble, she would beat us with the keys or anything in her eyesight. Big mama would whoop us with a dish rag when wet, which was the worst. She would always blame me for everything and send me upstairs whenever we got caught doing something wrong. One day one of our older cousins came over, and he set the garbage can on fire, and all the boys ran, and I got caught hiding under the table, and Big Mama tore my butt up with them keys. That's one whopping I'll never forget. She would always yell, "Sarah, get your stinky fast tail yourself up the stairs, Sarah." Big Mama didn't play about them boys; they were her favorites.

Around age five, two of my boy cousins who were two to three years older than me at that time, touched me in places they shouldn't have. Not understanding that it was wrong, I allowed it to happen and I never told on them . I was young, and I didn't know better. One of my boy cousins would always have me touch his private parts and play with mine. This happened with three of my boy cousins until I turned around eight years old, and that's when I knew it wasn't right. Scared of how I would get beat if my mama and Darla knew, I never said a word. Never did it result in them having sex with me or anything like that, but the touching happened often. I genuinely believe now that I'm older, that played a role in why I grew up so fast, as the older people would say. As we grew older, I never held it against them; we just behaved as if it had never happened.

Darla caught one of my boy cousins taking off my clothes while I was sleeping, and she whooped both of us. She swung me around and around by my arm and beat me with a belt. She had a very heavy hand. Darla was big and mean at that time. She literally would try to beat the hell out of me. She even would sit on my head sometimes so I couldn't run and just beat me with a belt and tore my little booty up. Don't get me wrong, Darla took excellent care of me, but when she did whoop me, which she did quite often, she didn't play. Lee would whoop me with house shoes and sometimes a belt, but it didn't hurt. When Darla would whoop me, she used belts, extension cords, and fists once I got older.

Around September of 1990 I attended Jensen Academy for pre- school. In Kindergarten, I had a boyfriend who was my boyfriend until second grade. He would get off the bus, meet me in the morning, and walk to school daily. I remember him fighting me in first grade. That's when the abuse began. One of my other favorite boy cousins, who I went to school with, took up for me and tried to knock him out, but he ended up knocking me out. I went to school with my twin boy cousins since Kindergarten, and I always looked at them like they were my brothers. They never came to Big Momma's house. I would always see them at school. They were my favorite cousins but were more like brothers to me. I had around seven male cousins who I grew up with and no girls. I had two girl cousins Slay and Ta- Ta who were two to four years older than me. I only saw them at church. Never really spent a lot of time around girls jumping rope, playing with dolls, dressing up, or doing hair. I was always wrestling and fighting with the boys or doing something I had no business doing.

Big Mama got sick and died when I was eight years old. Big Mama sang and read the bible with me the night before she died. I think she left her blessings on me. When Big Mama died, my Mama Lee was left with the house, and that's when everybody left. Darla moved downstairs, My mama Lee lived upstairs, and I stayed upstairs with mama. A few of my older cousins still lived there, but that was no longer the house where everyone lived. Some stayed, but many left. Sometimes, some would come and live for a while, but eventually, everyone was gone except one or maybe two here and there. All my cousins there were much older than me, so now I was the only child. Loneliness started to kick in.

Sometimes, Mama would keep the girl next door, and I would have somebody to play with. I had all the toys but few people to play with. I always had imaginary friends, and Darla's boyfriend, Donald, was like a big kid. He always played with me and took me to all the fun places. He called me, "show me." He said he called me that because I always wanted to show him something. I never got the chance to go outside and play. It was always school, church, and home I went to. Mama was very religious, and she took me to church with her every Tuesday night for bible class, Wednesday for prayer, Thursday night for saving the children, and Friday night for youth service. Saturdays were choir rehearsals because I always sang in the choir, and Sunday was the longest. We had Sunday School at nine am, Worship Service at eleven am, and Missionary Service at four pm. We didn't make it home until ten pm sometimes on Sunday, but that was my life, well at least until I got old enough to break free.

I didn't have anyone to play with at home, and even when we went to church, I would hang with my other older male cousins there because my older female cousins were mean, and they would always be in their room with the door closed because they lived upstairs from the church. One of my older boy cousins used to make me pay him two dollars to come upstairs. He was mean, too. The school was where I used to do all my playing because I was finally around some kids my age, not just boys but girls, too. I had friends who, most of the time, became enemies, which is truly the story of my life. Sometimes, my best friends were my enemies first, but then we became friends. I think I fought every girl in my grade in different years. They all said I talked too much, or I used to think I was all that. Maybe I talked too much. After all, I didn't get much attention at home or have anyone to talk to. When I would talk to mama and my sister often, they would say, "ok, now you're running out, so much for that." I wasn't good at communicating because I never had many people to communicate with. Growing up, I felt very lonely. Not only was I lonely, but I felt rejected and abandoned. My mama and father didn't want me; that's how I felt.

My dad Marcus was in jail for robbery. He got out for doing one bit and went right back. Marcus and my cousin went on a robbery together, and she snitched on him when she got caught. He went down when I was two years old with a fourteen-year sentence to prison. After doing all that time, he still got out and went right back. Carrie came and went a lot during my younger years. Carrie would come and get me and take me to garage sales and buy me things in the suburbs. She would take me to beaches and ponds to feed the ducks. We would always do free things, but it didn't matter then. I just wanted to be with her. Carrie's racist adopted father died one year after she gave me up for adoption from a heart attack. Carrie's adoptive mother and family blamed her for it. They blamed her because she had a black baby, but, in my eyes, it was the hate that man had in his heart for people that killed him.

Carrie started getting high off heroin after her father died because she felt guilty and shamed, she says. Carrie used to steal from her adopted mother to get the drugs. I know they thought Carrie was a real devil. Marcus told me she was a devil worshiper. He says they were riding around one day, and she had a devil toy in her car. And he threw it out the window, and it came back in the car. My daddy lied so much that the story was just so hard to believe. My trust issues started at a young age. Carrie would call and say she was coming to get me, but she never showed up. Instead, I would sit in the window counting the cars go by, telling myself she's going to be the 30th car, and then after the 30 cars ride by after counting, I'd say she's going to be the 90th car and counting 90 cars go by and the day turns into night Carrie never comes. I was always the little girl in the window because I could never go outside.

Carrie ends up having more black children with three different men, all cousins off the same block who lived in the same house. Carrie had my little sister first after me. Before having her, Carrie would come to get me for holidays, and her racist mom finally accepted me, but she would always make racist comments. Carrie's mom was harmless, a nervous wreck, I would say, but still racist. When Carrie would bring me around her mom and their friends, Carrie's mother was so embarrassed of me, and she would tell everybody I was Carrie's friend's daughter. Carrie's mother never told anyone I was her granddaughter. I watched her not claim me, and Carrie would cry and yell and scream at her mom for doing it. Carrie was always very friendly to me but always very sad about how her family treated her because of me. She was broken, lost, and confused too. That was very hard for me to witness growing up, and I didn't understand why.

After Carrie had more children, she eventually stopped coming to see as much. My little sister was their princess when I went around them because she didn't look as black as me. Even though she was black, things were different. My little sister would get all the gifts, and I didn't get much anymore. Next came my brother, and he was a drug baby. All of Carrie's kids after me were drug babies; I was the only one who was not. I would watch my little brother jump around the house like a monkey out of a cage, laugh, and be so wild. It was scary to watch him act out like that. I didn't understand what was going on here. I was well-kept and protected from the outside world, so I was never exposed to drugs and things that weren't normal. Then Carrie had another boy who was her miracle child prematurely when she was five months pregnant. He was in the hospital for a long time with tubes plugged up everywhere on his body, but he made it.

At one time, Carrie had all three of her baby daddies living with her. Right now, to this day, she still has two of them living with her. One of them was my last little brother's father, and the other one was my little sister's daddy, who would never leave no matter how badly she treated him. Carrie's mother always cracks jokes and says things like "slavery isn't dead in Carrie's house!" and that would crack her up. She always had corny jokes. Carrie always made my little sister's dad do everything cause my little brother's daddy couldn't do anything but scratch his stinky butt.

Talk about weird? This has been one of the worst things I've ever seen. I was always so embarrassed about this; it was just another confusing element of my life. Eventually, I wouldn't say I liked going with Carrie because she never had any food in her house; nobody ate at her house. She had two men there, all like the *Walking Dead* because they were high. Carrie would go to sleep standing up all the time; it was sad, and her baby daddy did too. They would scare the living hell out of me. I didn't know they were high when I was little; she lied to me about everything and told them they had sleeping disorders. School was the only place where I felt normal, even though I stayed in trouble.

In school, I was brilliant and even placed in gifted classes growing up until second grade. I was always on the honor roll and one of the top students in my class. My conduct and listening grades eventually got the best of me. I would always get a C in listening and an F in conduct or maybe a D, but that didn't occur until after gifted classes were over in second grade. The real trouble began in second grade, which was the year Big Mama died. Our teacher had suspended my favorite twin cousin, and after school, he chased him and threw rocks at the teacher while everyone ran behind them and laughed. I wasn't there to see it, but when I got to school the next day, they told me I had laughed all day. I thought that was so funny until I didn't. The teacher had failed me on a test we took that day, and I was so mad. I started to laugh and say things like, "You better run, Forrest, run," and everybody else laughed too. Another girl must have said something to him, too, because before I knew it, we were handcuffed together as we walked out of the school to go to jail.

With tears running down my face, I was so embarrassed because I didn't even do anything, and I knew Darla was going to kill me. Bebe, the girl who cuffed me, just laughed and said come on, girl and she thought it was so funny. That was Bebe and I's first real encounter together, and I will wait until I tell you how we reunited later in life. Bebe was my ride-or-die when we got older. Darla came to the jail to get me with a look on her face that if looks could kill, I would be dead. Well, I guess you know what happened after that; yep, she beat me like a slave.

Third grade came, and I had one of the prettiest teachers ever. She was tall, light-skinned and pretty. She always thought I was her favorite. I was shaped up just like her. Tall, pretty, and light-skinned, my sister Darla kept me in pretty clothes and shoes. Growing up,

I had a few insecurities because my nose and feet were enormous. I was also super skinny and tall and not too fond of it until I met my third-grade teacher. Ms. C was a model, and she started putting on school fashion shows for me to model at. The modeling built my confidence, and I was now getting all the attention I had never gotten, so this was great. Carrie disappeared for two years during this time, and it put a hole in my heart; no matter how much Darla and Lee did for me, there was always a part of me that didn't feel worthy or valued because my mama didn't want me.

Modeling truly changed my life. I modeled for churches and my school, and I did this until ninth grade. Darla had put me in a modeling agency in seventh grade, where they taught me how to do the catwalk, makeup, photography, and acting. Darla and Lee were so proud of me because I would be a star. In 1998 my mama and sister invested so much money in me learning to model and traveling to Hollywood, California, to compete in competitions against girls worldwide. I was awarded an honorable mention medal for acting in drama. They knew I would be the next top model, and my life changed.

Chapter 3:Once A Good Girl Has Gone Bad, She's Gone Forever!

No weapon formed against thee shall prosper, and thou shalt condemn every tongue that shall rise against thee in judgment. Isaiah 54:17

I use to Model for 1 year and half

I can't make this up. Some of the deadliest things have happened to me. It all started at a young age. Elementary school was now ending, and I was headed to high school in year 2000. From third to eighth grade, I was modeling and dreamed of being a model/actor and a lawyer. Mama and Darla had put me in the best private school on the west side of Chicago. I was accepted into Providence St. Mel. I always seemed to be very popular everywhere I went. I became well-known as a freshman in the entire school. I bonded with the varsity cheerleaders and the varsity boys' basketball team. I grew up with all the boys, so I got along better with the boys because I had never been around girls.

I was a virgin, and I knew because I hung out with so many boys that people thought I was having sex, but I wasn't.

It wasn't until January of the year 2001, my first year in high school, that I started having sex. I had been talking to this one boy, and I stole my sister's credit card and bought him a whole Coogi jean outfit out of Fresh Wear for Christmas, and he ended up cheating on me with my ex-best friend. My sister found out, and she beat me and blackened my eye. I was so embarrassed that I ditched school the next day. I had a new boyfriend Issac, who was four years older than me, so I decided to run him. The first day I ditched school was the day I lost my virginity. Not understanding sex, I just did it because it made me feel close to someone finally. I think I sang the songs playing on the radio the whole time. "Seems like a ready girl. Are you ready to go all the way?" That was the song I remembered being played at that time. He remained my boyfriend for six months before I left him for cheating on me. It's unbelievable how I started off having sex to escape the pain I was feeling.

As time went on at St. Mel High School, the dean of students, the boys' basketball coach, placed me on a strict contract requiring me not to have any social contact during hallway passing time. They said I was more interested in the social aspect of school than the educational aspect of school. I would get expelled if I was caught talking to anyone in the halls. Do you know what happened after that? I was expelled for talking in the halls. That was the first school I was kicked out of at the end of my first year. I was forced to attend a neighborhood high school where it all started. Not having siblings in the home or many people to talk to growing up, my mouth would always get me in trouble.

After being sheltered all those years, I was now about to be introduced to this cold world that Mama and sister tried so hard to protect me from. I was always in the window watching my friends outside, but I could never come out. I went from church to school. I went to church Tuesday night for Bible class, Wednesday night for prayer, Thursday night was save the children, Friday night was youth service , Saturday Choir Rehearsal, Sunday 930am Sunday School 11am Worship Service; sometimes, it would be all day on Sundays. Growing up, I thought my mama was so cruel for doing this, but now I was about to find out why they did it.

Walking to school through the 2800 blocks daily to go to summer school was like walking through another planet. I call it another planet because they were all like aliens down there. They were nothing like any other people I knew. My new public high school was six blocks away. Walking to school was where it all started. I was introduced to Hollywood, and I'm not talking about the one in LA. Hollywood was located right off the 290 expressways. A hundred guys were on every block, and they were all trying to talk to me. I was like fresh meat to them. It was all kinds of different people I had never seen, like crackheads, robbers, murderers, gang members, and so much more. It was action on the corner from where I lived, but nothing compared to down there. It was like the movie *Paid in Full* in that first scene when everyone was hanging outside, but it was worse. There were at least thirty people on every corner you turned, and it was at least thirteen blocks.

I got to know more people and started seeing all types of things happening before my eyes. I ended up getting a best friend named China. China was short and dark-skinned and had a charming sex appeal about herself. She was a part of a huge, well-known family down there. China was so fun to hang with. We didn't hang down in the jungle too often; we always took long walks outside the neighborhood. We would always get so much attention. All kinds of boys and men would stop and try to talk to us, but we were high class. We would only talk to boys who had money. They had to have nice cars with fancy rims, clothes, and jewelry, or we wouldn't look their way.

Remember I told you how strict my mama was? Well, that all came to an end one day. I would sneak my friends into my house to have sex with their boyfriends when my parents were gone. One day, my friend's boyfriend told me to run away from home, and if I did that, they would be so worried that they would never make me stay home again. That's precisely what I did one day: I ran away. They were so worried that they stopped making me stay home, but they also stopped caring for me. They said it was tough love, but it pushed me out to the streets even more.

China and I knew all the guys with the money and nice cars. They would love to ride around with us and give free liquor and weed all the time. When one car left, another one would pull right up. I knew my neighbors thought I was selling my body because there was always a different car outside blowing the horn for us to get in and ride with them. We met a lot of cool, friendly people until China decided to start dating a man from off Cali. She was my best friend, and we went everywhere together. Now she was hanging in Hollywood, and I'm hanging down there too. This is where it all went wrong.

I had three other friends who lived on Kedzie Street with me then. They were always super-fast. They were having sex at eleven and twelve years old, maybe younger. One of my friends was sleeping with multiple men at one time. The other two were sleeping with each other and always had a different boy to have sex with. I would be a good girl if I weren't doing what they were doing. At the time, I was, but I still had so much to learn that I learned the hard way in the long run.

In my opinion, I have always been an adorable and caring person. I never felt like I was buying friends, but that's exactly what I was doing. I remember my sister buying me all these designer outfits, and I used to bring all the new girlfriends to my house to see all the beautiful things I had so they would accept me, but they used me, talked about me, and plotted on me and never accepted me.

In the summer of 2001, I saw all my clothes on other girls, some of them I didn't even give to them. My clothes were just being passed around. Doing this only made them hate me worse. I always had more than most growing up. Spoiled rotten, I can honestly say, but that was the last shopping spree my sister had taken me on. My sister said she was done because I was misbehaving and giving the clothes away.

I walked around and passed out my modeling pictures after my sister always told me not to do that, but I went against it. I was so wrong. I wanted people to be happy for me and love me, but it only caused more hate and secret animosity. I was green and so dumb to the streets. I learned everything I know right now the hard way. Experience has always been my best teacher. Growing up confused and sheltered only made the street life harder for me.

In the Summer of June 2001, I met a man named Ice. He had to be around twenty - two years old. I had already seen Ice multiple times and thought he was attractive, but he had never even seen me, maybe because I was so young then. He was very dark with curls, and he talked fast and smoothly. I guess he had a way with his words. It was just something about him that I loved so much. Maybe it was the promises he made when I first met him or the way he would call and talk to me all day and all night every day. Ice took a trip about three weeks after I met him in California. I found it so attractive that the whole time he was there, he spent his time talking to me on the phone for hours. He intrigued me, and that made me fall deep in love.

I was only fifteen years old. I didn't have a clue what love was. I guess I was just fascinated with how charming he was to me. Ice was eight years older than me. He was twenty-three years old, and I was fifteen years old. I think I lied and told him I was seventeen, but I was still too young to be involved with a grown man.

In July 2001, my life started to change right before my eyes. The once young, innocent church girl/

model was about to start turning into someone nobody could even describe. Not having a fundamental understanding of sex and what it meant to do it, I began to make some terrible choices. There was this guy I had seen around Ice maybe once, but I didn't think they were friends because I didn't know either of them then and didn't know anything about taking my time to get to know a guy before I started to like him. I don't want to make excuses for all my behavior, but I feel you should know my circumstances at that time. I was the only child with nobody to talk to about the birds and bees. I had to learn things hard because I was never a good listener. My mama always told me that a hard head makes a soft behind. I didn't know what that meant, but I understand it now. Some things I never understood until now.

July 4th, 2001, Bird tried to talk to me and asked me to ride with him. I had always seen him in nice fancy cars with rims, and I thought he was just my type of guy; even though I had been talking to Ice on the phone daily, I didn't think I was doing anything wrong. Right? Well, maybe I was wrong.

I mean, I wasn't in a relationship with him or anything, but I guess we were building something because what I was about to do ended up breaking his heart. Bird asks me to go home with him. At the time, I had only been with one person. I got in the car with him, and the song Differences by Ginuwine was playing, and without even thinking, I said yes. I told him I wanted to try something new and went home with him. The sex was good, but it wasn't all that. I told this boy who called me his sister what I had done, and he called Ice immediately and told him what I did.

Song Cry by Jay Z was one of the hottest songs that summer. To best describe the moment, Ice called me about what I had done and Song Cry lyrics would best describe the moment. "A face of stone shocked on the other end of the phone. Word back home is that you had a special friend. "At the song's end, he said, "Once a good girl goes bad, she's gone forever." I'll never forget how that made me feel. Ice came back from California and wouldn't say two words to me. It was over. I thought to myself, I broke his heart. I'm unsure if he was heartbroken in real life because how could he be so hurt about what I was doing, and he had a girlfriend and a new baby at home? *How could I break the heart of someone who was involved with someone else?* Yet, I blame myself for everything that was about to occur.

The boy I called my brother who had told me name was Tdog. He was now shooting his shot at me, and instead of me never speaking to him again, I decided to give him a chance. China was dating his friend, and they had a great bond. I thought I could have what they had with Tdog, but I was wrong. It came nowhere close to what they had. Growing up with such a big family and being more street-smart than I was, I never would have thought she would have let them take us to the Shamrock Motel. Everyone laughed and teased me about it and even called me the rock, and I didn't even have a clue; they had taken us to one of the worst motels in the world. That was so embarrassing to me. *Why would they do that?* I didn't last too long with Tdog because my first encounter pulled up on the block while Tdog was shooting dice and asked me to come to the car . And I went, and Tdog said he was done. I guess I broke another heart. I didn't even do anything! At least, that's what I thought, but they all felt different. I had broken three hearts in less than three months, and they all knew each other. They treated me like the worst person ever walking the earth.

I still attended church often, but not as much as I used to. In September 2001, my church had a revival, and a pastor attended the church that year as a guest speaker. He saw things before they happened as if he was a prophet. He spoke all these things to people about themselves that nobody knew but God.

Prophet Robert called me up one day and told me some things in my ear that I knew nobody knew about me then, so I knew that I should heed what he was about to tell me. Nothing terrible had happened to me yet, but maybe a few fights, so it was very hard to understand what he was about to tell me then. He told me I would have dreams and visions. He asked me to spin around and around. While I was spinning, he told everybody how many times my life would change. Keep spinning, he said to me as I was spinning; he told everyone to keep their mouths off me while my life was changing. He spoke boldly in my ear and said, "You shall make it!" He repeated it over and over until his words were stuck in my head and my heart. He told me I had power in my hands and even had me lay hands on someone, and they fell out. He said I would even have a powerful testimony like Junita Byum. At the time, she was a compelling speaker under TD Jakes, and her testimony was so significant. She was a big deal. In my head, I was thinking, Who? Me? It couldn't be, but now I was about to witness exactly what he was talking about.

A couple of nights later, in that same week, he had everyone get on their knees and pray because he had seen thousands of caskets falling from the sky, and we needed to pray and intervene and bind the Devil, and it wouldn't come near us.

A few days later, on September 11, 2001, planes were hijacked and crashed into a building, and thousands of people lost their lives, but it didn't come near us. The prophecy had started to be fulfilled. A few more days later, my life had taken the first turn for the worse. September 14, 2001, was one of the many days I would never forget. Tdog and I had a bad argument one day because he had started seeing one of the girls I used to go to school with, and he thought I would be mad. I was a little mad, and we were arguing badly, and I bent down to pick up a bottle, and he threw a brick at the ground, and the brick broke in half and backfired and knocked me flat out in front of everybody. An ambulance was called, and I was taken to the hospital on a stretcher. My self-esteem had always been low, but it was ultimately out the window. My modeling career is over. I had two black eyes, and my face now had seven stitches right above my left eye. I thought I was the ugliest girl in the world. I was embarrassed and so hurt. Confusion was at an all-time high for me at this point because now, what am I going to do?

There was this girl named Karma, whom I had met previously. The first time I saw her, she was walking around looking for somebody with a butcher knife, saying somebody was spreading rumors about her tricking off for $100.

Another time I saw her, I used her Nextel chirp phone to call Ice, and she had his number already stored in her phone. I asked her how she knew him, and she replied, "That's my friend." I never thought about it because I didn't care or was just very naïve. I saw her again at the Park District swimming pool, and the boy I guess she was in love with was there. Shorty was attracted to me. He was tall, light-skinned, and very handsome, but light-skinned guys were never my type. He would always chase me every time I saw him. It didn't matter who was watching; he was on me bad. I would always run because I wasn't used to a man like that. Plus, I was never interested in him. Karma was a beautiful girl to me. She is light-skinned and short. She was talented. She could dance, she knew how to dress, and she could braid hair well like the Africans. She was someone I thought was cool. She had that hood girl swag I always wanted because I was half-white with no rhythm. I didn't have that swag, and she pretended to like me until she didn't.

Karma was the first person at my house when I came home from the hospital. She came as if she was trying to be a support and felt terrible for me, but now, I feel like it was all set up. She asked me to walk to her house with her. Karma lived in Hollywood, and I went with her without hesitation. With two black eyes, here I am, walking outside with stitches in my face. Ice popped out once we made it halfway to her house. He hugged her and told her this was my redbone. She is a real redbone in his voice. "You're ugly now." My heart shattered into a million pieces. *I'm ugly now,* I thought to myself. So sad and lost, guilt and shame had now taken over me. My life would never be the same.

After that, the bullying got worse. Halloween 2001 was one of the worst days of my life. I was traumatized. Everyone was outside in Hollywood that day; they were out throwing eggs, and I knew not to go down there that day because earlier that morning, I was out with the older girls, and they had thrown eggs at me and were shooting paintball guns at me. I ended up riding with some guys who lived down the street. They rode down there, and someone spotted me in the car.

They blocked the car off, and over one hundred people began to bombard the car. The guys I was with were scared and weren't about that life. They let them drag me out of the car, and they did me worse than in the movie Carrie. I had red hair in my head at the time, and they all took turns throwing eggs, milk, sugar, flour, beans, potatoes, salt, juice, pop, shit bags, and whatever else they could find. They all attacked me. It was one of the first and most humiliating things that ever happened to me. I remember walking with my head down with the red hair in my face soaked and wet. They beat me out of my shoes. They hit me with everything they had and ended the egg war they had all day with me. I looked like I was covered in blood. I never saw a human person get treated the way they treated me. They drowned me with everything they could find to the point I was not even recognizable, and NOBODY HELPED ME! Only one boy had enough sense to bring me my shoes because I was covered in everything in the kitchen. One of the first of many worst days of my life!

Chapter 4: Lost Little Girl

Yea, though I walk through the valley of the shadow of death, I will not fear; Psalms 23:4

Ja Rule dropped one of his best-seller albums that year. I was always in love with music. Music was my first love. Music always knew how to describe what I felt then and played a significant role in how I lived my life. Bad things had started happening to me. The boys would jump on me on every corner. The girls hated me and always made fun of me. I was being bullied every day by different crowds. They picked on me consistently. They laughed at me; they teased me. They would do things to humiliate me in front of big crowds with over 100 people watching. They would hit me, kick me, slap me, drag me, and sometimes even strip me out of my clothes. They would surround me and taunt me and say a lot of bad things about me as if I was the worst person to ever walk on the earth. *Where was my help?* It seemed like nobody cared, and no one ever stopped them from treating me that way. I was only fifteen years old. I was a baby. I couldn't imagine anyone treating my children like that because they would have to kill me first, but it just seemed like no one even cared.

Instead of someone coming to help me or stop people from doing me like that, everyoneblamed me. They asked why I'd keep going down there, but my school was down there; how else would I get there? I felt defeated. Where else would I go? I became addicted to weed and liquor to try to escape my pain. I was being abused every day for at least one year straight. Ja Rule dropped the song Ecstasy in the summer of 2001. A group of older girls from Hollywood eventually started to help me. They stopped all the younger girls from jumping on me all the time. I began to hang out with them because they were fun & dangerous. They wouldn't allow girls to mistreat me. That didn't stop the boys from hurting me whenever they got the chance, but it stopped the girls. I would ride around with the Demons, as they called themselves; they were super cool and fun. I'd get high and drunk with them and get into clubs with them. They were like the big sisters I never had, and even after they started doing me wrong, the respect I have for them will never change. Loyal to a fault, I'd even say.

The Demons would always be dressed to impress, and their hair was Shobb, as the older people would say. They would pull up on different blocks and get money and drinks and wherever else they wanted from the niggas on the block. I learned a lot from them, ladies. They were popping Ecstasy pills that year, and they looked like they were having the time of their life. I lied about my age to them, and they thought I was seventeen. One of the worst demons of them all was like a gang chief who had just come home from jail for stabbing another girl. She was one of the ones who took me under her wing, and her name was Bella.

Bella never let me get in the car with her on the days I wouldn't go to school, and she always tried to steer me in the right direction in a tough love way. When they'd pop pills, they'd never give them to me. I always wanted to do it because it looked like everybody who did it felt so good. Ice was in and out of my life, using me for sex whenever he wanted it, and at that point, I allowed it because I didn't even know who I was anymore. I was lost. Ice would pop a lot of pills. He would sometimes pop seven or eight pills, and he was rolling, as they would say. He began to give all the boys my age pills to pop, and now it was like my whole environment was doing it. I was one of the first young girls my age to do it.

The first time I popped a pill was in November 2001. I went with this older guy, the first to be kind to me. He took me to a nice hotel with a jacuzzi, he gave me my first pill, and we had sex. I didn't even know I was high. It was like the feeling was all in my head. Whatever I felt before the pill was like the feeling was enhanced. When he dropped me off, he gave me $500. It was like Christmas to me. Nobody had ever been so kind to me. I didn't even feel like I deserved it because I was convinced I was wrong. You would have thought he would have been someone I liked, but I didn't like him the way I should have. The guy's name was Mario. Mario was as heavy as they say in the streets. He had lots of money, and at that time, I was out there bad because my sister was no longer taking care of me because I wouldn't go to school, and I was forced to take care of myself at fifteen years old.

I bought some nice things to wear, and I was out looking good. Guess who's back? Ice! Ice took me to a hotel where he bagged up drugs and made me help him and never gave me a dime for doing it while I watched him pay everybody else.

He had sex with me, and he took my clothes and left me in the hotel naked with no money, no clothes, and no shoes on the south side of Chicago. I was forced to ride the bus and beg to get on for free with a sheet wrapped around me. I called my mama, and she was always there the best she could. She had to come to get me from Cicero & Cermak because the bus had ended the route and stopped, and the next bus driver wouldn't let me on. It was plenty of nights I had to call her to get me because I was getting left all over the place. You would have thought I learned my lesson and that I would change, right? Wrong! The drugs had utterly taken over my mind, and I had no sense of direction. I was dangerously in love with Ice, and he completely took over my heart, mind, and body.

All in one year, Ice had already done so many terrible things to me, and all I did was blame myself. I felt I deserved to be treated like that because of what I had done. He put cigarettes out on me, he beat me, he made other boys and girls jump on me, he left me places naked, he put me in a trunk and put a dog on me, he teased me and abused my mind, and I'm sure it was so many other things he had done that I don't even remember.

Long story short, he tortured me all the time. After I started popping pills, I started to get some courage, and I started to do crazy things because now I was getting fed up. I started stealing my mother's car because I still wanted to be outside drinking and smoking, but I needed some protection. I have so many questions for my younger self. I don't understand what I was honestly thinking. *Why didn't I leave that man alone?* Everyone told me how much Ice hated me, but I was convinced by the vibes we shared when we were alone that he loved me, and I made excuses for him. I would always say he was heartbroken and didn't know how to love me because of his pride. I always felt he was embarrassed to show his love for me because now I was labeled a hoe in the streets. Whatever people said about me, I accepted it as my truth. Ja Rule dropped the song lost little girl, which haunted me day and night. The lyrics expressed, "she could get a man to do anything but she is a lost little girl, this sexy thing is only 17 and she is a lost little girl."

Not knowing my worth and who I was or loving myself, I began to self-sabotage. Never feeling valued since birth and constantly dealing with rejection and abandonment issues, I never felt like I deserved to be loved, especially after my mom and dad didn't even want me. Like my sister told me, I believed nobody wanted me without knowing what she was saying. I was worthless, and I felt that way for years. I was lost in a world with no love, nobody to care for me, and no guidance or discipline. I was hardheaded, and I didn't even love myself. It was hard to love myself when I felt like nobody else did.

In 2002, I was arrested at school in April for carrying a knife. It was two weeks before my sweet 16th birthday , and they had put me on house arrest. I'm big on birthdays because that was the day I was born, so I took it real hard, and I had no peace in the home. They didn't understand me, and I didn't feel loved by them anymore. They blamed me for everything that was happening to me, and my sister acted like she didn't even care. I let them down and disappointed them, so they washed their hands of me in my eyes.

How can I blame them now that I'm a grown woman because I had stolen from them, disrespected them, and disobeyed everything I was told? They never explained to me why I shouldn't do the things they said they shouldn't do, and they said I do it because I said so. With little to no understanding of anything and a heart full of pain and feeling alone, I began to turn into a monster. Addicted to drugs and alcohol at a young age, I started to do things that I now regret.

On house arrest a week before my birthday, I stole my mother's car. My mama called the police on me, and one police officer knew precisely where I was. He was a pervert. He was mad because I wouldn't date him. He was sleeping with other underage girls around me, and he would always try to get me, but I wouldn't say I liked the police because they never did anything to anyone who ever did things to hurt me. He pulled up on the block and arrested me. I was sentenced to sixty days in the juvenile detention center. I spent what was supposed to be my big, sweet sixteenth birthday in jail. One of the worst birthdays of my life. I cried all day. I suffered from anxiety at an early age, and I would have the worst panic attacks. I remember hyperventilating very severely that day. I suffered panic attacks back-to-back, and then I got news back home that two people I had known were dead, and they were having their funerals the same day as my birthday. It was a sorrowful day for me.

I know you think this should end my troubles, but this was only the beginning. I turned into a nasty girl. While in jail, I always looked at Cosmo magazines, and they talked about sex a lot. I had never given anyone oral sex. Now I had learned everything about it. I came home at the beginning of June and was on probation.

I was super healthy-looking and had gained weight. I was always super skinny all my life, and once I was released from custody, I had finally gained some weight in all the right places. Ice was super thirsty to be around me, and like a dummy, I felt for it. Love can make you do some crazy things, or maybe it was the lack of it. Ice asked me for some oral sex, and I did it. The next day, I got his name tattooed on my back. All the young girls were getting their guy's name tattooed on them, and I was so messed up in the head that I thought Ice was mine. Ice had them drag me into the hallway so he could see it, and I couldn't believe his eyes. I had outdone myself this time, I can genuinely say. What was wrong with me? I promise you I do not know. I think I just wanted to be loved. Later in life, it made sense to me, but it never really made sense at all. I knew in my heart he loved me and would be my husband one day, but everybody thought I was just crazy. Yet the crazy thing about it to me is why did I even still want him?

Chapter 5: The Bottom

Job 13:15 Though He slays me, yet will I trust him.

After getting Ice tatted on my back, I thought things might improve. After being tortured, beaten, and jumped on for almost a year now, things only got worse. The man I thought I loved and who never showed me any love was about to do things that changed my life and how I felt about myself forever. Ice had said he threw piss on me a couple of times. He would see me coming down the street, and he ran and pissed in a bottle and threw it at me. As if the piss wasn't enough one day, he decided to pay someone to pick up some dog shit and put it in a cup for him. I had gotten his number from his cousin and called him one day.

The last time I was with him, I had heard his other baby mama playing on the phone with him, saying she got his number from the other baby mama, so when he asked where I got his number from, that's what I said. I told him your baby mama gave it to me.

I'm not sure why he got so angry or what caused what would happen next, but it completely broke me and took my pride. He paid one of the boys to come and trick me out of the house.

The boy acted like we were going to ride, smoke, and drink. He ended up having me buy the weed, and he bought the drink, and he pulled up on Ice's block, and there were over thirty people outside. I jumped out of the car and started running, and he had four boys chase me down, and one caught me. Ice ran over to me and knocked me down to the ground, and as I tried to lift my head, I saw him with some black leather gloves on. At this point, I thought I was about to die.

As I turned around and lifted my head, I saw him stick his hand with the black leather glove in the cup, and he slapped me. I didn't know what it was until someone screamed, "he just made her eat dog shit." He had slapped me with some dog feces. I jumped up, and I began to strip my shirt off and whip my face. The smell made me sick to my stomach. Everyone was laughing. I jumped up and ran with no shirt on and was crying. My heartbeat was racing, and my chest was beating fast from running. And in a state of shock at the same time, I saw a boy I knew, and I flagged him down and jumped in the back seat.

This was the most embarrassing thing. At this point, I didn't want to live. I ran into the house and told my mama and sister, and it was like they didn't care. They always blamed me for the things that happened to me. They would say, "Well, you shouldn't" of being down there. I went into the bathroom and bleached my face. It caused such a lousy irritation that one side of my face turned a different color. I ran to the police station, and they laughed at me. They kept asking me to repeat myself, so I ran out. I got a knife and tried to split my wrist. The knife went in, and it hurt so bad I couldn't even take it across my wrist. Bleeding from my wrist, I went and got a towel to wrap my arm to stop the bleeding. I walked around the corner to my cousin's house, and they didn't seem to care either. They just got me drunk and told me to calm down. I was in a rage. I wanted to kill him! I wanted him to die that night!

I got so drunk that now I was losing my mind. It was a girl who lived upstairs from my cousin who used to talk to Ice. She came and tried to encourage me, but it didn't seem genuine. I had asked my cousin to let me see her car, and she told me no, but she gave it to the girl upstairs to go and talk to Ice to find out what happened. At this point, I was ready to fight everybody. I began to argue with my cousin about how she could treat me like that, and she tried to fight me. Can you believe it?

The people who are supposed to love me and have my back saw I was hurting and now are trying to hurt me, too. She was a fat girl, and she started running up to me, and I had to run from her big ass. Then the girl came back and started saying what he told her, and now I was ready to fight, and we fought. Her dad and brothers refereed the whole fight while my family did nothing but try to break it up. After I beat her in fighting, she got a bat and tried to hit me with a bat, but I got away. My family didn't really have a clue what was going on, they thought I was just drunk and crazy.

Suicidal, lonely, broken, unloved, unvaluable, and uncared for is precisely what I felt the next day. My cousin got married that day, and I went to the after-party. Sitting in one place with my head down, ready to die and unable to look people in the eye anymore, I felt dead walking. My biological father's mother, who's my grandmother, said she was going to help me. She told me to come and stay with her, and she was getting me out of that environment before they killed me. Granny took me into her home. Granny had a lovely big mansion in the west suburbs. Granny was a real lady who taught me things nobody had ever taught me. She took time to teach me how to clean and care for myself. My aunt took me shopping at Von Mauer and bought me a whole new wardrobe, and things were turning around for me. I was enrolled back in school and getting back on the right track.

September 1, 2002, I got baptized at Living Word Christian Center and accepted Jesus as my Lord and Savior, and I received the holy ghost that day. When I went down in the water and came back up, I received some power. I felt something in my hands that

I could not even describe. It was like an electric shock or wave I felt running through my hands. I went into the spirit room where we asked God to fill us with the holy ghost, and they told me to start to utter the 1st words that came to my mind, and it was baba shada, and instantly, the words just began to flow on their own. It was a power I felt that I can't even describe. The lady walked by and said you got it! I received the holy spirit that day.

I began to start having dreams. I dreamed every night, and sometimes they were so bad. One dream I will never forget wasI was in my granny's house, and there were evil spirits in there, but she would pray and throw the oil, and they would disappear. The more I sinned, the stronger the spirits got. They got so intense that I ended up at my mama's house one day. I was downstairs sitting on the couch, and there was a man there who looked like Ice, but it seemed to be Joe Tory, an actor at the time. In this dream, there were two of me. It was me and another me in the dream.

The man began to make me this big offer about how he could give me the world if I just came with him. The other me went, but I tried to run out the door. When I made it out one door, the door to get out was locked. When I turned back around, the man morphed into a black hoodie with no body and red eyes. This image didn't have a mouth, but he was laughing, and I slid down the wall, and he said, "I got you now!"

As a result, I woke up crying. It seemed so natural. Shaking and afraid, I ran into my granny's room hysterically. I told Granny my dream, and she said, "Just go back to sleep; that isn't nothing but the devil." She prayed for me, and I went back to sleep. A week later, an unknown call came through on my phone. I answered the phone, and it was Ice. I was shocked. So many unanswered questions. *How did he find me? How did he get my number? What did he want?* I thought he hated me. Ice was telling me he had a proposition for me. He asked me to go to New Jersey with him. He would put me in a position that would benefit both of us. He said he wanted to tell me more, but we needed to meet and talk face-to-face. He picked me up from school the next day and took me to this man and his girlfriend's house, where he had a room for us to stay in. He never told me about it once I got there; he just wanted to have sex with me and spend the night with me.

He kept me there for three days. I knew my granny was about to kill me and worried to death because I hadn't talked to anybody, and nobody knew where I was. I finally returned home to Granny's house, and she was infuriated. I was in big trouble now, and out of the three months I had been there, I had never done anything like that. I wasn't drinking and smoking anymore, and I was going to school like a sixteen-year-old should. She threatened to put me out if I ever did anything like that again.

A few weeks later, I got a call from a friend in the neighborhood. She was the only person I kept in contact with from that area. She called me and said Ice had gotten his baby mama's name tattooed on his arm. *Why would she do that? Why would she interrupt my peace like that? Why did I even care?* And I cried like a baby. I went and lay in my granny's bed, and I just cried and cried; I felt so stupid. I was walking around with this man's name on me, and he went and got someone's name on him. I shouldn't have been mad,I can't tell you why, but it hurt me. I told Granny I wanted to get some money to remove his name from my back, and she told me to go downstairs and tell Grandad. So, I went downstairs to tell Grandad what had happened.

Grandad was sitting on the couch, looking weird, like he was high. I sat down on the other side of the couch, crying. He asked me, "What's wrong?" I told him Ice got a girl's name tattooed on him, and I just wanted to remove his name from my back. Grandad took out a rubber band wrapped around the money and got up, and he walked over to me and said here, take this. He gave me the money and said, "Don't tell anybody and I'll give you whatever you want." I was so confused. I asked him, "Don't tell anybody what? About the money? "He said," Don't tell anybody anything!" Then he bent down and kissed me on my lips. It felt very awkward because he had never done that before, so I'm lost now. I didn't think anything of it, and I wouldn't have made a big deal of it, but then he bent down and kissed me again, and this time, he tried to stick his tongue in my mouth, and it turned my stomach. I pushed him back, and he knew he had done something wrong by the look in his eyes. He repeated to me not to tell anyone, and I said OKAY.

I went upstairs, and I lay in bed with my granny still crying. Granny was reading and studying the Bible. Contemplating in my head: should I tell my granny because I didn't want to hurt her, or should I stay quiet? It was unbelievable because that morning, Granny had just told me a story about someone she had known. The girl's stepfather had been molesting her and told her he'd kill her if she told somebody, and he ended up killing her.

That put a lot of fear into me because I didn't know what to expect if I told my granny what happened. I had to tell her what happened because she was my granny and I loved her. I told her, and she was ready to attack him, but I begged her not to. I asked her to keep it a secret because I feared what might transpire after he was exposed. It hurt my granny and put her in a complicated space. Granny didn't say anything that night like I had asked her, and we went to sleep like a regular night.

I tried to go on with the next day at school like nothing ever happened, but I couldn't. My stomach was so weak I ended up throwing up. I ditched class later that day and found some weed to smoke because I never knew how to deal with the pain I was feeling, and I just wanted to be numb. I went home after school, and Granny told the family. Some believed me, and a couple said I was lying about him. She called Grandad to confront him when I arrived, and he said I was lying and had to leave the house. Granny said, "Well before she goes, I'm going to take her to the police station and let her tell them the story." Grandad didn't come back to the house. Granddad knew I wasn't lying, and if they had tested me for DNA because he stuck his tongue in my mouth, it was a possibility that he would have been found at fault and could have possibly been placed in jail. Grandad didn't come home for weeks, which made my granny sad. After weeks passed, Granny said that granddad had to come back home, and he was cooking Thanksgiving dinner, and I'd have to be ok with him. I decided I couldn't do that, so I called my mama and asked her to get me because I no longer felt that was a safe place.

Of course, many people said that's what I wanted to do, but I didn't. I couldn't stay in a house with a grown man who had done something like that to me, and I didn't know what he was capable of following. I loved living with my granny; that was one of the best things that ever happened to me. *Why would I give it all up to return to the struggle?* I was back in the trenches, but at least I felt safe at home. My home life wasn't happy because my mama was so hard on me. She tripped about the phone, and she was very strict, and I couldn't have any company. My mama and my sister were mean, and they yelled about everything. They were sweet at heart but very impatient when it came to me.

Back in the trenches, I was. Back hanging out and getting high off weed and drinking liquor every day. Drinking and smoking helped me cope with life and my problems. It helps me be numb to pain and gives me the "don't care" attitude. I didn't care about much, not even myself.

Months went on, and now it was Feb. 10, 2003; my friend Kay went with me to meet Mario. Valentine's Day was coming, and I wanted to get fresh, so I decided to see him. Mario was the only man I was dealing with who was willing to help when needed.

We ended up chilling with him and his friend. I didn't know that my friend had even known his friend, but she appeared very comfortable with him. We popped pills and had a drink, and we smoked. Now we were feeling groovy. Mario decided to pull up at a hotel room, and I was hysterical because I felt it was very disrespectful to pull up to a hotel without even asking Kay, but I guess that's what Kay was used to. The fact that he pulled up to a hotel without even making sure it was okay didn't sit right with me, and I snapped. or I could have just been high and tweaking off the pill.I had him drop me off, and guess what? Kay decided to stay with them. Some friend Kay was, huh? The next day I came to her house; she had been shopping and happy and had some money, and I just knew that my so-called friend had backdoored me for my nigga. Well, he wasn't my nigga, but he was the nigga I was sleeping with. *Why couldn't she find her own?* Kay was very promiscuous, and she had no problem with sleeping around. This alone should have taught me a massive lesson about friends, but I still didn't learn.

I was very upset about what Kay had done, and I knew that Kay and Karma were sleeping with the same boy, and he liked me, so I knew if I even went and kicked it with him, it would make them both jealous. On Feb.11, 2003, I went to Rockwell Garden projects alone. There was always a party over there, and I wanted to go.

I got over there, and the boy that both of my fake friends liked was there with his baby mama and daughter. It didn't stop me from kicking with them because there were a lot of people in his house, and they had the music loud with plenty of weed to smoke and alcohol to drink, and he even bought me some food. That day was the 1st day I had ever eaten steak. So, we were kicking it and chilling, and Kay walked through the door, rolling her weed and asking, "Is this what you on?" It was never my intention to deal with Mario. I just wanted to make her mad, which I did. She ran out of there, and I sprinted behind her, and she disappeared. I don't know where she went. I wasn't familiar with the projects and had only been on them 2x before. I headed out of the building as high as I could be. A crowd of girls across the street in front of another building called me. I wasn't about to stop for them; they were mean and loved fighting. I was by myself, and there were over ten of them.

I crossed the bridge and walked through the park to the street. Karma lived across the street from the park, next to the homeless shelter. Someone had called Karma and told her I was heading her way. From afar, I saw Karma approaching me, wearing all black. She wore a black T-shirt, a black leather jacket, jogging pants, and some black and red retro Jordans. She appeared to be alone with a butcher knife, headed towards me.

I could talk to her, but that didn't work. Karma walked up with the knife in her hand, screaming, "Where have you been?" I grabbed her and tried to tell her he was there with his other baby mama, but I ended up saying his baby's name instead of her mother's. She tried to snatch away from me, and as we wrestled with the knife, someone approached me from my blind side unexpectedly, and it took me by surprise. "Let her go," he said! I looked to my left to get him off me, and Karma snatched away, and the knife went up my face. I went down and screamed, "You just stabbed me!" She stood there in shock as if she didn't even know what she had done, and I immediately began to attack her. I know the angels of God had to be with me because I remember her swinging that knife over ten more times. I only got stabbed one more time in my face . As I dragged her by her hair, she began trying to stab my feet, but she didn't get another chance to cut me again. She was covered in my blood. I was bleeding out. A stranger walked up and begged me to let her go. "I want that knife" is all I remember saying. I did not want her to keep the knife she cut me with. Whoever the person was told I was going to die out there if I didn't get medical assistance right away.

A trail of blood is all I saw as I ran off. I looked back, and she was walking slowly with her head down, covered in blood. I had a blood trail down three blocks. I saw some boys I had grown up with and asked them to give me a gun. I was going to kill her now! They begged me to get help. Blood was everywhere. I couldn't feel anything.

My adrenaline was rushing, and all I could think about was murdering her. I ran another block to the house where Kay's grandmother lived and our other friends across the street. They were screaming and crying and scared to death. Kay walked in and immediately started crying. Half of my face was hanging, and blood was everywhere. The ambulance came, and they wrapped my whole head up. I cried, and I screamed. I didn't want to walk outside like that because everyone would see me. It was another one of the most embarrassing things that happened to me.

I went to the hospital, and my mama came. All she would ever say to me is "why were you down here? This wouldn't have happened if you hadn't been down there." Not much sympathy was given or much concern in my eyes. My biological mother and her boyfriend came to the hospital after I got out of surgery. I had almost two hundred stitches in my face up across my ear to my head. I would shake badly because I was in a state of shock. I was just stabbed in my face. I once thought I was one of the most beautiful girls in the world. My life was over now in my eyes. I didn't want to live, and I didn't have a clue what the future even holds for me at this point because I was all alone in a world wanting to kill someone who had family and friends, and I was alone.

My mother's boyfriend handed me a cigarette to smoke, and I smoked my first cigarette in Mt. Sani Hospital's bathroom. On Valentine's Day, I was released from the hospital and could go home. I went outside to the liquor store and saw Ice outside the store. He screamed, "She should have killed you B****!" It's over for you!" At that point, all I wanted to do was die again. I walked around with my head down. I was at a point of no return. I knew I wasn't a killer at heart. I feared a lot of things. I'd never seen the world so cruel. I started doing drugs even more now because I was no longer the person I was. I was a monster.

My face was full of scars, my heart was full of pain, and my mind was completely gone. I started smoking leaf with one of my neighbors down the street. I wanted to be a killer. I heard that my cousin would smoke leaf and kill people. I tried to do it for a week, but it wasn't my thing. The man that I was stabbed over never showed any sympathy. He came to get me as if he wanted to talk to me, and he took me back to the projects and offered to give me one thousand dollars not to talk, and I didn't want it. All I was thinking was, *is he serious right now?* Only one thousand dollars for my face! He said the lawyer would only want five hundred for the case and would give it to me instead. There was a boy there, big black and ugly, who told him just to give him the thousand dollars and he would kill me. Super scared wasn't even the word, but how I was feeling right now, death wouldn't have felt more effortless than living because this was hard.

"Many men wish death upon me! Blood in my eye, dog, and I can't see I'm trying to be who I'm destined to be, and they are trying to take my life away. I put a hole in her for messing with me, my back in the wall; now you're gone see that you better watch how you talk when you talk about me because I will come to take your life away."

This 50 Cent song was the hottest song at the time, and it was unbelievable to me how whoever was the hot new artist at the time always had a song about things like what I was going through. He had a verse that said, "Slim switch sides on me let her ride on me, I thought we were cool why u wanted me to die homie." Music was the only thing I felt like I had. By what they were singing or rapping about, I felt they understood my pain, my situation, and what I was going through. I always used music to escape my reality. I could relate to the music. It was a way to communicate how I felt.

Karma turned herself in, and when the police called me, I was high as Stone Mountain. I didn't know if I was coming or going. All I wanted to do was catch her and kill her. I felt like she deserved to die for this because I didn't deserve this at all. The police at Harrison and Kedzie police station questioned me as a minor at sixteen years old by myself alone in a room. They asked me to tell the story a hundred times. I had no adults in the room with me. They made my mama and granny stay in the lobby. They began to bring up my criminal history and what I did wrong compared to hers because she didn't have a criminal record. They labeled me a troublemaker, and they didn't seem to care about what had just happened to me. When I mentioned her brother was there, they told me they had to hold me in custody as well for investigation, and I snapped. The last thing I was about to do was sit behind a wall and lose my mind even more. They charged her with a misdemeanor and let her out of the police station; she never even reached the county jail. This was my face that was stabbed. Nobody cared, is all I could think. I hated everybody!! I lost all respect for the police, the world, and myself. I hated myself the most.

How could I let this happen to me?

This can't be life! (tears)

I think I died at least twice in my lifetime, if not more than that.

Chapter 6: Dancing with the Devil

Yea, though I walk through the valley of the shadow of death, I will fear no evil. Psalms 23: 4

No longer knowing who I am, as if I had ever known who I was, I was hopeless. My life was over. I didn't want to live, and I was afraid to die. I'd wake up, leave right out the door, and never return until it was time to sleep. Lost, confused, and ready to learn how to be a killer, I was a mess. I was so depressed and stressed. I no longer had any sense of pride or dignity. I felt like I was dead walking. I wouldn't look people in the eyes, and I stayed high and drunk all the time. I needed help, but no one thought it would help me. I was too far gone. This was the worst I had ever felt in my whole life.

This lady thought she would walk around and live comfortably after almost taking my face off. She had another thing coming. I dropped out of school and was now on the streets more than ever. I had to take care of myself. There was nothing normal left in my life. I thought I was a monster. I didn't look normal, and I didn't act normal. Life for me was over; at least, that's how I felt.

By May 2003, one of Ice's friends had returned home from jail. I had slept with Ice maybe two weeks before his friend Mo came home. No matter what Ice did to me, whenever he called, I always came running with no questions asked. I was either blinded by love or a damn fool. I think it was both. I don't even think I know what love is to this day. Ice was controlling my mind and manipulating my heart. I didn't even care because I felt like I deserved it. Nobody ever treated me like I was special or like I was someone. My mama and daddy didn't want me or show me I was unique or loved.

Mo and I became friends because he had been sleeping with my fake friend Kay. I caught that fake friend who betrayed me before, now betraying me again with Ice. Ice was also sleeping with Kay now. I'm not even close to being in my right mind; here I go again, moving off emotions; now I'mdrinking, walking, and talking. We walked from liquor store to liquor store for hours and hours. We were vibing.

I thought he was a good friend. My heart always seems to make a fool out of me. It got late, and I was intoxicated, so I asked Mo to walk me home. The house he lived in was horrible. It was so nasty it was the worst house I had ever seen. The walls were gray; the tub was black; the carpet was so nasty that it was unbearable to live in and smelled disgusting. There were roaches and rats everywhere. If you sit on the couch, rats would run past your feet and behind your back. Feeling sorry for how he lived and always having a passion for helping people, I invited him into my house. I snuck him into my room because Mama didn't play that. I could never have any male company ever. The type of males I dealt with, I understood precisely why she didn't want them around, but she never even knew who they were; it was just never allowed.

I made Mo a nice comfortable pallet on the floor with blankets and a pillow, turned the fan on, and went to sleep. Mo woke me up on top of me, choking me and squeezing my nipples so I couldn't scream. I wanted him to come and see how obsessed I was with Ice and go back and tell him with hopes that it would make him see how much I loved him. I had his pictures that his mom gave me on my wall with his name. Instead of Mo seeing the love I had for Ice, he saw an opportunity to take advantage of me. He forced himself on me that night, and I was raped.

Later, I found out I was pregnant. In such an insufficient space in my life, at a point I did not want to live, now I'm pregnant by a man I didn't even really know. I chased him with a butcher knife and tried to stab him because this wasn't supposed to happen to me. Now I was over-lost in the sauce. What was I going to do with a baby? I didn't believe in abortions, and I didn't want to carry a child for nine months and abandon it and give it up for adoption like my mom did me. Guess who's having a baby at seventeen years old? Me!

However, the pregnancy was a gift to me. I was young, and it may have been the wrong time for many people, but it depends on who's asking. I had lost all hope for life. The unborn child I was now carrying gave me something to live for. I was not in a relationship with his father, nor was the child conceived out of love, but it was just what I needed at the time. I fell in love with knowing I was about to be a mommy. Somebody who loves me for me. I knew it was going to be hard, but I wanted my baby, and I didn't ever want to make my child feel the way I had to grow up. So, it was time to step up to the plate, and I thought I was ready.

I was now four months pregnant by a man I barely even knew. My mind was still in an awful space, and I was still stealing my mama's car despite her calling the police on me every time. One night, my friends and I were riding and having fun like we do.

We saw Karma outside with her friend and her daughter. She was walking right across the street in front of my own eyes while I was driving, but she was with her daughter. I wasn't a killer at heart by a long shot. So many things went through my head. I wanted to run her ass over! My heart wouldn't allow me to do such a thing to her with her child. I couldn't hurt a kid, and it took a lot for me to hurt anyone. I just wasn't the type of person to want to hurt people. I love people, and I enjoy helping people. I didn't have the heart to hurt people, but I had to learn how to hurt the people who had hurt me or were still trying to hurt me.

I knew how to make her mad. I screamed out the window, and we approached the stop sign where they were. "Where's your baby daddy? Tell him I'm on my way," and I pulled off real fast, and we turned the corner going toward the projects where he was from. She was infuriated. We laughed and went on about our night, having fun as usual. As the night went on, we were just out having fun, and I got a call from Karma telling me to pull back up like she wanted to fight, so we returned to our hood. She was standing outside with two of her friends with bats. My friends were younger than I was, and they stayed ready for that action, so they all jumped out of the car immediately without hesitation. I pulled off to find some bottles because I was not running up on her again without anything in my hands because she always fought dirty. As I was looking for bottles, a few demons pulled up, and I asked them for a bat. When I told them why, they told me to come on; they would make her put the bats down.

The demons hopped right out of the car and did just that. Now they were disarmed; I jumped out and ran right up. I had a butcher knife, and I wanted my lick back, but my baby daddy's niece was with me, and she wouldn't let me stab her because I was pregnant, and she kept telling me I was going to go to jail so I gave her the knife, and I ran up on her. Karma maced me, but it didn't stop me from beating her ass. Blind with mace in my eyes, I grabbed her and hit her over and over, and my young gunna beat one of her friends up, and the other one ran. Pregnant and maced, I began to get tired. As my strength was weaker from not being able to breathe from the mace, Karma bit me in my face. She bit me so hard, I went down to the ground. She thought she was about to get the best of me, but my friends grabbed her off me immediately and threw me on top of her. As soon as they threw me on her, more people in favor of her came and broke it up. Not only did I have two scars on the right side of my face, but I also had her teeth marks imprinted on my face from her biting me so hard.

Nineteen years later, you can still see the bite mark. I wanted to kill her now! Every time, she was always trying to do something to scar my pretty face. Once Karma saw that more than half of the hood was now riding with me, she stopped coming out so often, making it harder for me to catch her.

Wintertime has approached, and I'm preparing to give birth to a beautiful baby boy. I started making changes because I was about to become a mother. I went looking for jobs, had an interview at McDonald's, and didn't get the job.

That wasn't very encouraging to me, but I kept trying. I had another interview at Best Buy right across the street from Mcdonald's that denied me a job. I guess what they say is true: if one door closes, another will open. I got the job at Best Buy, which was way better than working for McDonald's. My favorite big cousin Big Boss, who was older than me and used to hang with my father, was now very concerned about me and active in my life. He was the only one trying to help during those very trying times. He had given me a car before but took it back, and now he has given me a van. It was a nice van with rims, and it was super cool. I was getting my life back on track and being responsible again, but some things never changed, like me dealing with Ice.

Ice appeared to be so heart broken when he found out I was pregnant by one of his childhood friends. He rode around for days listening to songs that appeared to me as sad or about being heartbroken. He never showed his emotions to me about how it made him feel, but I just knew because I felt like I knew him. He was young, full of pride, and very egotistical. He cared a lot about what people thought of him, and the last thing a man on the street wanted to say was they were in love with a hoe. They created that label for me, and I eventually started to believe in myself when girls were doing far worse things than I had done.

I knew I didn't do the things I witnessed other girls do, but I guess I still wasn't carrying myself as a woman should. My baby daddy has now gone back to jail after only being out a few months. Ice became more relaxed with me while I was pregnant. He was always trying to use me for something, even if he didn't need it, because he was addicted to having that power to control me. I let him get the van my cousin gave me while I was working. One day, I woke up, and the van was gone. I called my cousin like somebody stole the van, and he said, "No, they didn't! I did." My cousin had taken the van from me because he heard I was letting Ice drive it.

A few months later, Ice went to jail, too. It was like karma was catching up to him. I was pregnant and working and starting to return to normal. On February 11, 2003, I gave birth to a baby boy. I wanted to name him Pimfunta after my uncle, but my sister threatened not to help him, and my baby daddy said he wouldn't claim him if I didn't make him Jr because that was his only son. I named him Jr. I had a beautiful baby boy one year later, the same day I was stabbed in my face a year before. I knew this was a sign that God gave me a second chance at life. Both years, I was in the hospital from Feb 11 - Feb 14. I came home from the hospital two years straight on the same day. I had him dressed so nicely. He was everything to me. My boy was so handsome and red. I had a change of heart, but it didn't last long.

Karma kept contacting me to apologize because she knew what she had done was wrong. In her heart, she knew I didn't deserve it, but the damage was done. Two months after I had my son, I got surgery on my scar to revise the way it looked on my face. The original scar was like a long centipede in my face from the side of my mouth to my head. Not knowing if Karma attempted to be my friend and if her apologies were genuine, I still allowed her the chance. She came to see me and cried in my arms, and she was very distraught about the situation. I just had a baby.

I didn't want to go to jail or continue at war with her. I was in a vulnerable headspace that she took advantage of at the time. *Was she sorry? Or was she just coming around to see who my baby looked like? Or how my face looked now after my first surgery attempt to start the process of getting it removed?* She snaked me before. I don't know how I could even be so naïve or stupid to allow this girl back around me. I always felt so stupid for not being able to hurt people or hate them the way they hurt and hated me. I was just different with a heart of gold. The way I was treated reminded me of the life of Jesus. How badly they treated him and how they hated him for no reason and tortured him. His friends betrayed him even to the point of death.

I was now on mommy time with a new baby, but still, my heart was broken, and no real revelation of who I was. I was still lost in the streets just now with more responsibility. Things started to turn for the worse a year after having my son. I started off selling weed, and one day, I found a rock and tried to sell it. I sold the rock to an undercover police officer after one of the boys told me not to do it. I was starving that morning, and I just wanted some food. I thought I had $10 to get food but was wrong again. I got in the car with this guy and had him take me to McDonalds, and the police surrounded the car and arrested me. I was released a couple of days later to house arrest, and I was fighting a felony delivery charge for one rock that I found on the ground as my first case. I was always hardheaded, and I never wanted to listen. The guys I was selling the weed for gave me three hundred dollars to bond off house arrest, but instead, I let one of the other boys tell me just to keep the money and break the band, so that's what I did. I wouldn't say I liked the police because they would always take me to jail for the things I did wrong, but nobody ever went to jail for all the things they were doing wrong to me. After experiencing so much trauma with no healing, things only got worse.

I broke off house arrest and had a court date soon. My mama begged me to go to court, and I didn't want to go because I was scared they were going to take me in custody, but they didn't, and I'm glad I did go. I was convicted for the delivery charge and given probation for two years since it was my first case as an adult; I was only eighteen years old when this occurred. I began to look for jobs again because my stepmother worked as a supervisor at the unemployment office, and she was able to help me find jobs with my criminal record.

I was in and out of school. It was my junior year, and I had been to over six schools in three years. I was either kicked out or I dropped out. It was embarrassing going to school and not being able to dress to impress, and once I was stabbed in my face, I no longer felt human, so I dropped out altogether. I went from job to job, never staying at any of them longer than six months. I was working for Portillo's Hotdogs, about forty-five minutes from my mama's house, and I was doing well. My baby was now a year old, and my sister was taking him to Disney World for the first time. I should have been excited because it was a blessing, but instead, I was angry.

I was angry because my sister and mama were going on vacation with my son, and they weren't taking me, and I couldn't stay home. They wanted me to go over to my dad's house. At that time, my biological father was incarcerated, but my adopted mama had been previously married to my sister's dad. They had me calling him my father, too. They wanted me to stay with him while they were gone. It was not bad staying with him, but it made me angry, plus his new wife was straight from hell. She never really wanted to see him do much for me. She was like the stepmother from hell. I never cared for her. *Why couldn't I stay home? Why did I have to go somewhere else?* I had already felt left out and couldn't even stay home.

Mama had no trust in me, and after dropping out of school and losing the chance to model, my sister seemed to have very little love for me. I know they had their reasons. I didn't understand life, and I always wanted to do it my way, which was a bad combination and a generational cure because my biological mom was terrible, too. I had stolen from them and brought people into their homes without permission, and I let them down because they tried their best; they knew how with what they had to raise me to be different.

My mama and sister were preparing to leave town that morning, and I stole my mama's car keys, but she had the car moved and hidden from me. My sister thought I was too scared of her to steal hers, but I knew they were about to leave, and they spent so much money on the trip. What was she going to do? I stole her car. She was so furious about it. I don't know how their trip went, but they were gone for seven days. I had the car, and I was happy. I slept in the car and rode around all day. Most of my associates were my age or younger and we were excited.

Do you remember Bebe, the girl I went to jail with in second grade? Well, Bebe and I were back jammed tight. I stole the cars and she rode with me. We rode to the suburbs to steal gas because you pump before you pay there. I would fill the gas tanks and pull off. We would sit down, eat, and run out of the restaurants without paying. We pulled up to clothing and shoe stores, and I sat in the car out front while she ran out of the stores with us some to wear. We were utterly outlaws, and it's sad because that's what we felt we needed to do to survive then. I couldn't go to work. After all, I knew my sister would have the police there waiting for me because I had stolen her car. We did whatever we needed to do to survive. Times were different back then, so there were always guys we knew standing on the blocks, so we would ride around and beg different people to keep a few dollars in our pockets. I was vicious out here and didn't even know it.

Chapter 7: Demon Time

" Then Jesus said, "Father, forgive them; for they know not what they do" (Luke 23:24)

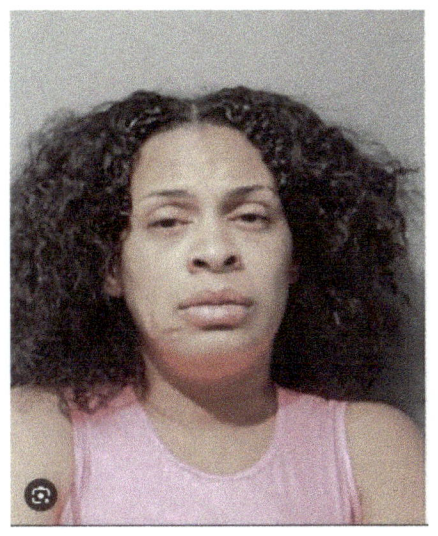

I went from Charity to Church! The streets changed my name once I became a valid member. I became a monster. I was no longer who I was born to be; I had become someone else. I proudly wore the name Church because it felt like the streets had finally accepted me. I was no longer the sweet, brilliant

Charity. I was a crazy chick named Church who didn't play. I had earned my stripes and became one of them.

I don't want to brag, boast, or make it seem like my actions were cool. That's not the reason why I'm here. I'm here to give you a testimony of what I survived and a front-row seat to the things I went through growing up. I'm not proud of these things, nor do I ever want to leave the impression that this was something extraordinary because it is not. I do not glorify the things I've done, and I'm embarrassed because it's not who I am. I learned so much from the struggle, and the things I've done, seen and went through don't seem normal or realistic, but I'm here to tell you everything I'm saying happened. I can't make this up. Some things were so gruesome that I don't even have the words to say, and it's impossible to include everything I witnessed in life, but I could give you a glimpse of my story. Now, let's get back to it…

A few days passed, and I was riding the wheels off my sister's car while they were gone. A few family members came out to chase me, and I led them on the biggest chase they had ever been on because one thing about me was I knew how to drive. Thank God nobody got hurt because I was going up one-way streets to escape them. I even led the police on high-speed chases and got away. I was fearless. I got a call that my cousin was shot, so I rode out west on his block to check out the scene, and here was my mama's car parked with a bullet hole in her windshield. I got my friend to drive my sister's truck, and I hopped in that car and pulled off because I still had the keys. Now I have both cars. I know my sister couldn't think about anything but killing me when she got back because she was already evil. I didn't care, though; I was full of pain, and I was trying to escape the life I was given.

We looked super cool to the people in the neighborhood because now I had options. I have two cars now. One of the days, she went into the stores and stole matching dresses, and we thought we were too cute. We had been out all night high off ecstasy, and it was now morning. Nobody had cars at that time; that was our age, so that's how we would hustle. We would take people to different places for money. Some of the guys asked us to take them to McDonald's that morning, and we did. It was a couple of the crazy girls from off the other side of the bridge inside. Those girls hated the girls from our end and were always fighting. One of them was super crazy and tough, and many people feared her because they knew she had a lot of family to fight with, and she knew how to fight well.

I guess we were both going through something that day because me and her got into an argument in the restaurant, and we started fighting outside. LL and her friend started jumping on me, and my friend jumped in to help me after the boys had to tell her to jump in. They snatched my dress and my panties off in broad daylight on the busy streets of Roosevelt and Kedzie, and now I was outside fighting naked. They took off their belts and chased me around the whole restaurant while I was naked, trying to whoop us. It was so embarrassing. I've been getting humiliated my whole life.

There were so many people out there just watching. I finally returned to the truck, and we jumped in and pulled off. While we were trying to get away from them, the girls kicked and beat all types of dents into my sister's truck. I knew she was going to kill me now. They chased us all that day in different cars. So many were popping up and trying to get me, but I knew how to escape those jams.

Two days later, my sister and my mama returned from vacation after being gone for seven days. Most days, they were gone; I slept in the car because I had nowhere to go. My sister had my cousin take me around to look for me, and when they found me, they chased me for about twenty minutes all around the city. They were running into the back of the car, trying to get me to crash. I was running lights and driving fast and crazy, and they were right behind me.

Finally, after I felt like I had gotten away, I was going so fast around a swirl that the car spun out, and we were literally two inches from hitting the pole. We jumped out of the car and started running, and they chased us. I had gotten away, but when I looked back, my cousin had a man with a bat chasing and hitting my friend, so I came out of hiding to help her, and she jumped on the bus and left me. The man beat my legs with the bat, and they called the police on me cause now I couldn't run and had me arrested.

Sitting in jail after I had just gotten beat with a bat was crazy to me, especially by my own family. I was released from jail with a court date later that day just to come home with all my clothes in garbage bags thrown outside because now I couldn't come back home. It was another one of the worst days of my life, and I had a lot of them. But this time I brought it on myself, I guess. I called my biological mom to get me and my son because I had nowhere to go. She had three other children and two men living with her, so I had no room to stay there long. Plus, we never got along. She'd always try to fight me or talk crazy to me when I had altercations with my younger sister or brothers. I felt accepted nowhere. I felt in my heart it was me against the world. My biological mom would get mad and put me out and tell me things like "that's why I didn't want you. I knew you weren't going to be anything." Those words hurt like hell. I didn't know who or where I belonged; nobody loved me. Those things alone broke my spirit and killed my confidence on top of all the evil things people were doing to me.

As time went on, I got worse. I didn't learn from my mistakes. I was addicted to drugs and alcohol. I was addicted to the streets because even though they didn't even like me, it was the only family I felt like I had. I was standing on corners selling drugs. I was having sex with different men who didn't deserve me. I did not love or value myself. Due to my circumstances, I tried to be the best mother I could be. I made sure I kept my son clean and fed. My mama wanted to leave him at home with her because she didn't want him out in the streets with me.

I started stealing cars from these men. A few times, men tried to leave me places because I wouldn't have sex with them after smoking and drinking with them. It was getting cold outside, and I had no money, no car, just nothing, so I started doing things I shouldn't have, especially as a young woman. It was hard to believe I was a young woman because I felt like a monster. Nothing had ever been normal for me, and there were never many people who really loved me, so it made me feel like I didn't deserve to be loved. I'm not making excuses for my behavior because I didn't even try to do better. I accepted this as my reality, and I lost hope. I couldn't see a way out, and I felt stuck.

I know stealing cars wasn't common for young ladies, but I made it a trend. I was stealing different cars every three days, and every time I lost one, I would get another one. I couldn't see myself walking anymore. My life was in danger, and I used cars as a shield, a getaway, and a way of survival. I had a ball just driving while listening to the music. I used cars to get from A to B because being without was not an option. I rode around and pulled off weed and pills from drug spots. I took everything because nothing was ever given to me. I began to ride with the boys because they had guns, and there were so many people looking for me to do something for me. I was never the type to set people up because that wasn't my style, but we robbed every joint on the westside of Chicago. We took everything in life because going without was not an option. I started to hang out with Bebe every day, and our goal every day was to try to take over the world like Pinky and the brain. She'd always ask me what we would do today, and my answer would be the same every day. We're going to try to take over the world.

I went to jail so many times. I was in and out of the county jail. Throughout my life, I had thirteen misdemeanors, four felonies, and over twenty-six arrests. This was not something to be proud of. It was very depressing. I contemplated suicide many times, but I always said I would instead let someone else do it. I wasn't tough enough to kill myself, and I wasn't as crazy as I seemed. I wanted to be crazy. I looked in a mirror and made myself act crazy because I felt that was the only way to survive. I look back now and wish I would've run. I always cared too much about what people felt about me. I never wanted to be known as scary. I wanted to be excellent. I wanted to be accepted. I wanted to be liked. I wanted to be respected, but no matter what I did to earn that love, I felt I was missing; I never got it.

The void remained. Unfilled, lost, broken, misunderstood, misguided and misplaced. It was hard for me growing up. I made terrible decisions as a young woman. I wish things could have been better for me. I was intelligent, pretty, and talented. I just knew I would be a model or a lawyer, but I turned out to be a gangbanger and a street woman. Something I'm sure my mama and sister never saw coming.

I started hanging out with these boys outside the neighborhood, and one of them was like a brother to me. He never wanted to see me on the streets stealing cars and selling drugs, so he took me in like his own little sister. My mama would call him if she knew I had stolen a car, and he would take it from me. He would let me ride his cars, and he would feed me and get me and all my friends high and drunk, and he would help me change my ways. A few years went by, and my brother was convicted of a murder he didn't even commit. He pled guilty to the gun charges, so they automatically charged him with murder because he was charged with the gun. They gave my brother over sixty years. Watching someone who finally showed me so much love was heartbreaking to be stripped of his freedom. "FREE WEZZY " Please save the Baby!

HE INNOCENT!!

I stopped stealing cars after my big brother took me in and taught me many things. I had been through so much over the years, from stealing cars. I dragged a state trooper one time; he reached into the car, tried to open the door, and went on a high-speed chase. I got away, but my friend, whom I always looked at as a sister, had to pee, and without thinking, I stopped in an open alley, and they found us. I was arrested for trespassing, fleeing, and eluding. Bebe was usually the one who was always with me if it wasn't my sister. My friend tricked some guy into taking her home, and we took his car one day. The crazy part about it was he knew where she lived. He went to her mama's house. Her mama, being scared and never really liked me, brought them to my mama's house. When they arrived, he caught the girl who dropped us off to him and fought her. He was so angry and violent. He dragged the girl out of my hallway and tried to fight her. Thank God nobody got hurt.

Most people got their cars back sometimes with damage, but there were a couple of times some people never got their cars back, and if they did, it was so damaged, they probably didn't even want it. I want to take this time to ask everyone to please forgive me. I'm sorry and regret everything I did and went through as a young adult. I wasn't in the right state of mind, and I wasn't myself. The devil was trying to destroy me, and I thank God every day he kept me. I shouldn't still be here, butI'm thankful. Only God could have kept me through the things I've been through. I give him all the glory; I know he is real because I tried him for myself.

My life of crime went on from seventeen years old until I was around 23 years old. Selling drugs, stealing, sleeping around, addiction, fighting, robbing, and scamming. I did it all to survive. I lost all hope, and I lost myself. I was not the little church girl anymore, but I knew God had a plan and purpose for my pain. I was betrayed by the ones I loved the most. It was never my enemies who hurt me; it was always the ones I called family or friends. I was arrested and took cases for people when I wasn't even guilty. I was placed in a seventy-two-hour investigation for a robbery I hadn't even committed, but one thing about me I never told. I was never a snitch. A boy even threw drugs at me that weren't mine, and I didn't fold on them even though I was about to be charged for something I was innocent of. I was loyal to my hood. The hood was never loyal to me, but I didn't allow it to change who I was.

Chapter 8: Church

"Nothing in all creation is hidden from God's sight. Everything is uncovered and laid bare before the eyes of him to whom we must give account." (Hebrews 4 13 NIV)

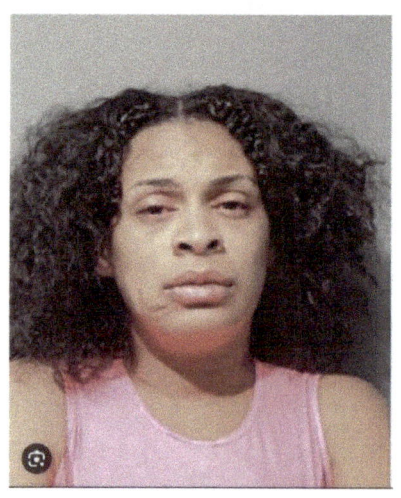

I had started messing with this boy, and he was so cocky and arrogant. It was nothing but sex; it wasn't a real relationship. He had a girlfriend, but I didn't know her, and I never valued myself enough to know I deserved better. People had conditioned my mind by how I was treated, and things were said to me that I was not worthy of love. After having sex with him twice, I ended up pregnant by this man. He didn't want me to have the baby because he felt like it was embarrassing to have ties to me, but it never stopped him from having sex with me whenever he wanted too. I contemplated getting an abortion because I already had one baby with no support from his father. I didn't want to do it again. I just had an abortion for the first time two years ago.

I was sentenced to one year in 2006 in a women's prison. When I came home, Ice was on me badly, but his friend Bird, who was the first person I had sex with while Ice was in California, was on me, too. I was so pretty and thick when I came home. I was cleaned up from drugs and alcohol, and I was looking good again.

110

They surrounded me the first day I came home. Ice made jokes about how they were about to party with me, but Bird wasn't feeling that. Bird told me to come go with him, and I did. When I jumped in the car with him in his excellent new Range Rover, he told me to tell Ice to get his weight up, and I told him, and we pulled off. I went with Bird, and he dropped me off back at home. It was cool, but I never connected with him like I did with Ice. Even though Bird always did more for me than Ice ever did, the connection wasn't there.

Later that night, Ice showed up at my house and refused to take no for an answer. Ice kept me close every day after, which was the most attention I ever got from him. We were together every day, and it finally seemed like it was something real, but he still had a girlfriend at home. After a month or two, I became pregnant by Ice. Ice knew it was his baby, but he told me I had to have an abortion, and it weighed on my heart. I knew I was scared to try to keep the baby because of what he might do to me. I had so much fear for this man because I had never seen someone so ruthless. I cried, and I cried, but I went to the abortion clinic, and he took me. We argued so severely in the office. He was gone when I went in to have the procedure done and came out. I was so high off the medicine I couldn't walk or see. I was so weak, and it hurt me so bad. By the grace of God, my biological mother was pulling up when I walked out the door. She wasn't always there, but she was always there when I needed her most.

Traumatized by the last abortion, I refused to get another one. This was my body, and I wasn't about to allow a man to persuade me to do something that hurt me so badly. Here it is, 2009, and I'm pregnant by another man who does not want the baby, but it was my baby, and it was my choice, and I was keeping him. I had been on the run because I didn't do the thirty days of swap. I was running from doing fifteen days in the county, so I had to leave my mama and rent a room in my sister's house. I was no longer on the block selling drugs anymore. I held the drugs, and I got paid for it now, so I wasn't on the corners selling packs anymore.

My second baby daddy was different. He still wanted to have sex with me, but he would say the meanest things to me as we got undressed. He would say things like, "I know that's my baby, but I'm not claiming it," and "Who wants to have a baby by a woman who jumps in and out of different cars and stands on corners acting like a rat." In fact, he said things to me like this all the time but then had sex with me immediately after. I started to think about everything he was saying to me, and it challenged me to want to do better because I wanted him to be proud, not embarrassed, that I was having his child. I knew I was about to have my second child, and I didn't even have a high school diploma. I went back to school and got my GED on the first test attempt.

My sister was tired of me and everyone always in and out of her house, so she decided she was about to move, and I had to find somewhere to go in thirty days. So now I had thirty days to find somewhere to go and come with the money to do it. My back was against the wall, and I had to do something, so I did some things I regret today, but I got the money I needed to move with, and I found my first apartment out south in the Mexican neighborhood. My baby daddy's friend was like my best friend. I hooked him up with my cousin, and they were a couple, and he got the basement apartment, and I got the second-floor apt. I stopped hanging on the corners and started getting ready to have my second child. I had another male companion who was always there for me when I needed him. He helped me pay the rent and ensured I always had a few dollars.

On February 3, 2010, I had my second child. My baby boy had me in labor for fifteen hours, but he gave me no pain. My boy wouldn't even come into the world until my mama showed up and started praying, and that's when he came out. My beautiful baby boy melted my heart. All I knew was I didn't want to leave him like I left my first child all the time. I wanted to be better. His father decided to see him after he was about a week or two old. My baby has been his twin since birth. There was no denying him if he wanted to. His father also had another woman pregnant at the same time I was. She was pregnant before me. She tried to punk me, but that never worked. I wasn't anything nice to play with.

Three months later, my child's daddy was sentenced to eighteen years in prison. Here I am, twenty-three years old, on the run with two children with no fathers. It was hard, but my mama was always there to help me when nobody else would. My biological mother was there for us the best way she could. My biological mother introduced me to the suburbs, where my oldest son always liked to be. He hated to be in the hood. I would take him to the hood, and he would always try to run away, and he would cry. He saw many terrible things and did not like that lifestyle. Some boys also tried to bully him, and he was not a fighter. And I couldn't stand to see my children go through the things I had too. I allowed him to stay in the suburbs with my biological mother sometimes during the summer and even went to school out there a couple of times while I was in jail.

I moved to Broadview, outside of Chicago, after living out south for a year. I was still on the run, but I didn't drive. For two years, I ran before I got caught. I walked back and forth for thirty mins every day to get to work and back home if my mama couldn't pick me up. I got tired of walking, and I decided to buy myself a car, and I went to jail that same night.

The door on the car wouldn't close, and I tried to drive on the expressway while trying to keep the door closed. I was pulled over, and all I could think of was I was about to go to jail. For two years, I had been sitting down and sat in the house with my second son Lababy for a whole year, and now I was about to have to leave him. All I could think of was that I was on my way to jail. I took the bottle from the back seat and started chucking it down.

When the officer approached the car for the second time, he smelled the liquor. He asked me to step out of the car and do the test, and I failed. I was so angry I was about to leave my kids again. I screamed, yelled, and cried. When I took my mugshot picture, I stuck my middle finger up. The picture went viral all over the state attorney's office. I spent two weeks in the county for the case I was running for and was released. The state trooper initially charged me with a misdemeanor because it was my first DUI charge, but it was upgraded to a felony.

Facing prison time with two children had me in such a terrible head space. I had everyone praying for me. My granny went to the courthouse right before my court date and prayed. She poured blessed oil from the bottom of the courtroom stairs to the top front door. It was so much oil when I arrived at the court the next day it was visible. We all went in and sat down, and they never called my name. They asked me who I was there for, and no records were found. It was a miracle. God had shown up and showed out. All I had to do was stay out of trouble and stop driving, and I would have been forgiven. I didn't do what I was supposed to, and six months later, I got caught driving again, and they brought the old case back up.

I knew I was on my way to jail. I lost my mind. I was doing things that I knew I shouldn't do. I would rather die than go to jail and leave my babies again. It was a week before I had to turn myself in, and I was on my way to a funeral. The night before the funeral, I witnessed a girl I knew of who had been shot over thirty times a year before getting shot over twenty times again and taking her last breath right in front of me. It was like she was trying to say something, and she started spitting up blood, and she was throwing her hand out as if she was begging for help, but she died. It was so heavy on my mind. I couldn't believe someone would shoot a girl down like that in cold blood over 20 times.

The next day, I went to a funeral for one of the guys who had been shot and killed a week before. We acted like fools on the way to the burial. We were a hundred cars deep, and we took over the streets. I took the other side of the street down Roosevelt, swerving left to right while all the cars behind me followed. We started at Roosevelt and Kedzie and went to Des Plaines before I crashed doing sixty hands with another car on the wrong side of the street. I saw it coming, but I did not want to stop. I didn't want the girls in the car with me to get hurt, but I didn't care what happened to me because I was on my way to jail in less than seven days. By the grace of God, nobody was hurt. The car was totaled. I passed out.

The boys came and woke me up and dragged us out of the car, and they said the lady I hit fell out and went into a state of shock because of all the people and commotion that was taking place at that time. I got to the burial and woke up. They scared me so badly, telling me that I killed someone. I cried and laid out on the ground because I couldn't believe this was happening to me. Helicopters were flying all over the cemetery, and every police station surrounded it.

They didn't arrest me at the cemetery, but they called my phone that night and told me they knew it was me, so I needed to turn myself in. I turned myself in the next day and was charged and released. Three days later, it was time to turn myself in to do eighteen months in IDOC. Usually, I run. I never turned myself in, but I was tired. I was ready to change. I wanted to be free from drugs and alcohol. I wanted to change and knew this time would only make me stronger. On April 24, 2012, I turned myself in to do my time.

Chapter 9: Til Death Do Us Apart

He who finds a wife finds a good thing and obtains favor from the Lord. (Proverbs 18:22)

On December 11, 2012, I was released from prison after spending nine months in ILDOC. I couldn't wait to kiss the ground when I walked out of those prison doors. While incarcerated, I got closer to God and attended some treatment classes. I learned a lot about addictions, why I was using drugs, and identifying my triggers. I was released a month earlier for attending drug treatment and good behavior. While locked up, I prayed every day in the spirit for twenty minutes a day and read the Bible. I made my requests to God that I wanted a new life, a husband, and a daughter, and when I came home from jail, that's exactly what I received. Next time, I know how to be more detailed about what I want.

I was happy to see my kids and family. I was overwhelmed with joy to be free at last. I made a vow to the Lord, which was my last time. I got home and took my baby to the barbershop for his haircut because I always wanted my boys to stay fly. As I walked down the street, everyone greeted me as if they really missed me; plus, I was back looking good today. Healthy, healed, glowing and thick. The squats and sit-ups I did every day were starting to show.

A car rode down along the side of me, stopped, and let the window down. It was Ice and my other street sister, Big Demon. She was smiling and happy to see me, and Ice was too. They asked me to get in the car with them. They had on Pelle Pelle leather coats, and they looked good. I got in and Ice and I began talking all night. We went over to Sis's house, where we kissed for the first time after sleeping with him for twelve years. I knew he was in love this time because he never acted like this before. It was like a dream come true. The man I loved the most was finally loving me back out loud and in public. We took a million pictures. I couldn't wait to show the world. I won! I felt like I accomplished something because I fought long and hard to win his heart and get his love. It was like everything I went through was finally paying off.

On my second day out of jail, Ice was already buying me things. He bought me a phone and a coat. He told me to find an apartment because my mother would never let him in her house. The next day, I went to see an apartment, and two days later, I had keys to a new apartment. I hated living at my mother's house because she was too strict for one, and for two, she had gotten old and could not keep the house like she used to. We always had giant rats because of the dumpster behind our house and the vacant basement. I had been through so much, and I didn't want to live there anymore, so I took the first place I could get as a convicted felon.

I was so happy. The apartment wasn't very nice, and it was on the third floor, but it was where I called home. Terrible roaches came from the apartments in the building, but we did our best to keep it clean and down as much as we could, but it was infested. My brother Church would always laugh and say you know this house wouldn't even pass the section 8 inspection, and we would laugh. It was mine, and I was just happy not to be at home with my mama; I had my two kids and the man I always wanted, on top of the fact I was free and got a whole apartment in four days of being released.

Ice and I fell deeply in love, and he always did anything for me. I truly loved him from my heart and saw past all his flaws. I loved him more than I ever loved myself. Christmas had come, and he did a lot for my boys, and now it was New Year's Eve. Ice had been on house arrest at his mother's house and was screwing around with the girl upstairs before I came home from jail. He had a couple of friends over, and we laughed and drank. I guess I had gotten too drunk, and we started arguing before I knew it he was dragging me around the whole house, banging my head on the floors, stumping me, and hitting me. He beat me for so long in that house in front of his mother, and that was the saddest part about it. I eventually was able to get my biological mom, Carrie, to come get me.

New Year's Day 2013 - Happy New Year! Everyone was saying, but I was crying because I had two black eyes and a lease agreement for one year with no job and two kids as a convicted felon. Some would say these were my self-limiting beliefs holding me back, but I'd say it was a fact, and this was my life. No matter what it looked like, I knew I could never return to my life of crime. Out of love and forgiveness, and my desperate need for help, I decided to forgive Ice and give him another chance because we were drunk, and he said he was sorry. Plus, *what was I going to do?* It was either that or the shelter. Carrie's house was already overcrowded, and my mama's house had just fallen apart and needed remodeling or gutting. I had forgiven him before, so I believed that he would get better, and I would always pray to God to change him.

We quickly became relationship goals because we made it against all odds. Plus, Mr. Prince Charming always knew how to make everything look good to people outside looking in. He tattooed my name on his chest real big with angel wings. Our love was deep, and he wanted to live in my skin. He went everywhere I went. He went to the beauty shop and the nail shop with me. He went to church and all my family functions. Besides the BS, he was the perfect boyfriend to everybody else, even me. We were working overtime to have a baby, and finally, I was pregnant. I didn't think this at the time, but now I do feel like he only wanted the baby out of spite because his last baby's mother left him while he was in jail, and he was hurt and wanted to hurt her. I wish I had known then what I know now.

Pregnant with a baby girl, and I was so excited because that's exactly what I had prayed for. We lived in each other's skin, so wherever he went, I would go, and I would ride on the side of him all day, just rubbing his face and playing with his ears until my baby came out looking just like his twin. The pregnancy didn't stop the abuse, and fighting continued. He had started to act differently while I was pregnant and leaving me more often now, and it caused problems. I'm just now realizing as I'm writing this. He was with me all the time out of love and insecurity. We had severe trust issues with each other. I came from being the other woman to his wife, and he knew all the dirty things I had done before we reunited.

Ice enters the door, observes me packing my clothes, and asks me where I am going. Seven months pregnant and sick of him leaving me, I told him I was done and I was leaving him. I'm here to tell you, ladies, never tell a man when you're about to leave; leave quickly and quietly because that was the day I almost lost my life and my child. Ice said, "you can leave, but you aren't taking that baby with you," and he stomped me down to the ground, kicking me in my stomach and hitting me over and over, trying to kill my unborn child. He banged my head to the ground so hard they had heard it on the first floor. They called the police, and Ice ran and got away. Scared to give the police accurate information, I only gave his first name. I packed my bags and a few things for me and my children and left them in an ambulance. I was taken to Mt. Sani, and the Lord knows I hated them. I called for my father to come and take me to a better hospital, and he came and got me.

Transported to Loretto Hospital by my dad, I thought I was safe. I left my bags in his car while I went into the hospital, where I was admitted for internal bleeding. In the hospital, starving, lonely, and scared, Ice continued to blow up the phone with apologies, not having an extensive support system. I told him to send me food there, and I began talking back to him because, honestly, I never felt like I really had too many people I could call on. I truly felt in my heart besides my mama financially - he was all I had. Starving for love and craving for attention, I allowed a man to mistreat me for years, all because I never felt worthy. God did it again! Three days later, I was released from the hospital, and my baby and I were OK. Thank God! That was indeed a miracle; if you had seen the horrific abuse I had undergone, you would understand.

My dad came to pick me up and take me to his home with him and his wife. I didn't feel welcome at all. She would ask me things like are you scared to go home? As if she wasn't looking at me, pregnant with two black eyes. Lady, you should have feared going home for me. I asked for my bags so I could shower, and suddenly, nobody ever saw them or knew where they were. I knew my dad was getting high, but I never thought it was that bad. All I had to my name was $50, my social security cards, and a few outfits to try to leave this abusive relationship, and the one person I thought I could trust betrayed me. My bag was gone. I felt defeated. All I wanted to do was go home. I lost all hope. I had nowhere to go, and my things were gone, and I was seven months pregnant with my third child. Ice had finally put some real fear in my heart because if you could do that to an unborn baby, I knew he was indeed a demon straight from hell.

Scared straight and lonely with no way out and about to give birth to my new baby girl, I took Ice back. Life was hard for me. I made so many bad decisions to hurt myself that I genuinely regret it today. Nobody had hurt me more than I truly hurt myself. Ice was always very remorseful about what he had done and always returned with a gift to make up for it. Many people had witnessed the things I showed them I was gaining from the relationship via social media, but nobody truly knew the fear and hurt that I felt inside. I was hopeless and scared that if I tried to leave, he would kill me. I was slowly dying inside.

On October 24th, 2013, I delivered a healthy, adorable baby girl within two hours of admission. The nurse called it a drive-through delivery because Charming popped out. No pain medications or anything. I had no time because Charming came out so fast. Her father was there and woke up for the delivery but had no knowledge of what to do or how to comfort me because he had never been there for any of his children's births. I had no complications, and I was now a mother of three.

Ice was there and helped a lot with our child, but my cousin died one week later after I had my baby. One of my favorite boy twin cousins was shot down in cold blood in Chicago's Street. I was devastated; I just lost my brother. I went into a state of depression that I could not even describe. I just had a child, and there was nothing I could do. When one of my other favorite boy cousins passed away over ten years ago, when I was in my madness, stealing cars, I would go and pick up all the killers in my neighborhood, and we would rob the joints. I wouldn't allow them to work on my cousin's block and he was gone. Now, things were different because after coming home from prison for the second time and having a new baby, I couldn't live as I used to.

A week later, we buried my cousin, and that was one of the hardest things I had ever had to do. I couldn't believe my cousin was lying here in the casket dead. I was hurt to the core. His twin brother had been in jail for almost all his teenage years for robbery, and he was not even there to see his brother one last time. In disbelief of what was going on, I stood in the back of the church after running out of the church because I couldn't take seeing him in that casket.

Bird's brother Church was like one of my right-hand men. Church loved the girls from Hollywood, and he would fight with us, let us ride his cars, and just a down for whatever type of nigga. He slid on the side of me and whispered in my ear and said "if I go before, you go. Don't let anybody come to my funeral with no rest in peace hoodies on and t-shirts. Bury me like the boss I am," and he looked at me and smiled. He said, "I don't plan on going nowhere soon, but I'm just going to tell you because I know you are going to stand on it!" I looked at Church and said if I go before, you don't let anybody stand over me and look down on me that didn't like me. He looked back at me and said, "Well, you know it's just going to be me and the preacher, right? What about your son, lil pimp? Do I let him in? because you know he isn't too fond of you either." We just started to laugh because Church was always funny as hell.

Every day, I dreamed of my cousin when I went to sleep. At first, I was scared, but then I was happy because I could still be with him in my dreams. Then it got scary because I started to see him rise from the dead, and that's when I begged him to stop coming to me. My other cousin, Lil D, was taking his death hard.

A couple of weeks passed, and Ice was discussing marrying me. I was excited and scared because I knew there were still some things he didn't know I had done while he was in jail. I thought telling him what I had done would build trust, and he would appreciate me telling him before somebody else, but that was not the case. Ice had gotten drunk one night and started fighting me and hitting me repeatedly in the same eye over and over. He choked me until I thought I was going to die and banged my head on the passenger window over and over. Sad to say, here I am again with another black eye raising my children. Scared to leave and terrified while staying with very little support and places to go, I endured it.

A couple more weeks passed, and my brother Church had been looking for Ice for a few weeks, but I never told Ice. I think the Church needed some money or some assistance because the GDs from K town had put a bounty on his head for the murder of one of their associates that he didn't even do, so I heard. I'm not sure precisely what truly transpired with him. They had shot him up previously but were unsuccessful in taking his life. He was always getting money from Ice when he needed it because Ice was older and like his big brother. I had a secret that nobody but Church and one other person knew. Scared of his loyalty to Ice, he would tell on me, so I never told Ice he was looking for him until one day I wanted to talk to Church and Ice was so possessive and controlling I knew the only way I could talk to him was if I tell Ice to call him because he had been looking for him. Ice called Church, and Church told him how he couldn't wait until he left him because he wanted his homie back, and Ice would laugh about how he would send a jet to pick up the next. They would always play and talk with each other because that's what we do.

Unfortunately, five to ten minutes later, my brother Church was dead. When we got the call, my heart skipped a beat. I just talked to Church, and he couldn't be dead. *How could this have happened to him? Why?* I was heartbroken that two of my favorite people were gone. Fly High Forever Church!! Rest in heaven, Boog! Gone but never forgotten. I love you all. Your names will live on forever. Two of my favorite people were taken from me within two months. I left the house to see his mother because now all three of her boys were dead. My heart goes out to her. Not only did my brother get killed, but he was killed in front of his son. I loved their kids like they were my own; if I got it, they got it.

You would have thought Ice would sympathize with me, but instead, he wanted to argue about why I was going to his mother's house. He wanted to argue with me after the funeral that he didn't attend about why I was going to the burial because he was at home sick. I thought he was super crazy. That was my brother! I loved Church. When Ice did me so dirty back in the days, I had a few homies that showed me love I had never touched before and always looked out for me. I did things that weren't right, but I was a gangster in these streets, and they respected me because I did things that thugs never did in the streets, and I never snitched. I had gained more love from the guys in the streets who respected me than from girls. There were a few of the Lady Lords who had respect and love for me, but they never came through like my brothers. Rest In Peace to all the soldiers we lost along the way, and Free the Rest!

New Year's Eve was approaching, and we had already paid for a trip to Vegas and had matching outfits made for that night. We went ahead and took flight, and after making love the first day, we got down there. Ice asked me if I would marry him while I was there. I said yes! We married on December 31, 2013, in Las Vegas. I picked our sanctuary, and we had a genuine service. We were picked up by a limo and taken to the church. I could send everybody the link to see our wedding live online. I marched down the aisle, which was like a dream come true. I was marrying the love of my life. Despite all the bad things he had done to me. I loved him. I was happy to be his wife. Out of all the women he had been with, and he was with a lot, he decided to make me his wife. We didn't have our rings yet, so we lit a unity candle together, and the preacher read this scripture –

1 Corinthians 13:4-7

New International Version

4 Love is patient, love is kind. It does not envy, it does not boast, it is not proud. 5 It does not dishonor others, is not self-seeking, is not easily angered, and keeps no record of wrongs. 6 Love does not delight in evil but rejoices with the truth. 7 It always protects, always trusts, always hopes, always perseveres.

In the King James Version, it reads –

1 Corinthians 13:4-7

King James Version

4 Charity suffereth long, and is kind; charity envieth not; charity vaunteth not itself, is not puffed up,

5 Doth not behave itself unseemly, seeketh not her own, is not easily provoked, thinketh no evil;

6 Rejoiceth not in iniquity, but rejoiceth in the truth;

7 Beareth all things, believeth all things, hopeth all things, endureth all things

That was a very powerful scripture to me because it wasn't just my name but also my life. I cried the whole service because I couldn't believe this was happening to me. I was the first to get married in my age group, and after all he had done to me, he was marrying me. I felt special and honored but also scared because what was I getting myself into? My love for him had me blinded to the facts.

We returned home as husband and wife, and I had so much faith in us that I knew things would get better one day. We had a lot of great times together, and he protected me from getting hurt by anyone else. He would go crazy if anybody ever tried to hurt me. He was a great provider and protector, but he couldn't control his emotions. We moved to the far west suburbs, which wasn't his idea, but I made it happen. I knew moving to the suburbs would suit my kids, and the police would come fast if needed, unlike CPD. I worked a job around the corner to walk to work every day. I never had to work; he would provide for us, but I felt I had to do things for myself as a woman.

I taught him so many things. I helped him get his license and his first job, even though he didn't keep it. I taught him new ways to live. I introduced him to God, and he received Christ as his Lord and Savior and was baptized. He was Muslim at first, but now he's a Christian. We helped each other stay out of trouble. We kept each other on our toes. We couldn't get along all the time.

Most times, we would argue over the dumbest things. We didn't have the same interest. He was an earth sign, and I was a fire sign. He was eight years older than me, and I still had a young, wild side of me that he hated and tried to control. I'm wild and free-spirited, and he wanted to be more ladylike, classy, and reserved. His message was right, but his delivery was horrible. I didn't have much respect for him because of what he had done to me all my life. It was hard for me to listen to him without feeling like I was being controlled or being a part of his abusive ways.

I'm unsure how many fights we had, but I know we had a lot. All the fights came when he was drinking. He never hit me one time while sober, no matter how hard we argued, so I always found myself making excuses for his behavior. When he got mad, he would take the things he bought for me away. He took my phone one day, and my kids heard us arguing. This was one of the first times my kids had ever got involved. My oldest son came into the living room and asked him to give me my phone back, and he yelled at my son, which caused me to snap.

This was the day he put fear into my kid's heart. He yelled at my son, and we started arguing. He told my boys how he would kill their fathers, and "their dads weren't nothing but cowards," he said. He told them how he would beat them up, too, if they played with him. He ripped down the Christmas tree and knocked the TV down, and when the TV fell, it hit my youngest boy. That was the last day my sons ever got involved in our altercations. It put fear in all our hearts, and we would constantly have to walk on eggshells to keep him from being mean to us. I begged my children never to get involved again and, if I screamed for help, to call the police.

He would always yell at the kids, and he wanted to be able to whoop them, but I wasn't having it. I watched him beat me all my life; I was not about to let him abuse my children, too. Those were my children, and nobody was going to mistreat them. He grew up in such a hostile environment where he was getting beaten constantly; he thought that was the way to raise our children. All he did was yell and be mean. He wasn't very family-orientated; besides, how could he give the kids something he had never seen himself? He didn't even know what love was.

Throughout the years, I have watched Ice change for the better. He wasn't all bad. He was charming and respectful to the public, and nobody would have ever known how he treated me behind closed doors. He would put on a whole different mask in public. He was very good at pretending to be something he was not. He had a good heart and would help everybody. Sometimes, I felt like how he passed out money gave him satisfaction or power. He would always pass out money to whoever begged and come home and cry about it, which was one thing that bothered me about him. He was unstable and sometimes unable to think for himself. We'd plan to go one way, and then someone else would tell him something that would throw off the original plan. It was like a dog chasing his tail. We were going nowhere together fast.

I got my family comfortable with him coming around, and then this happened. He beat me on the side of my cousin's house while they were all inside for a party. He beat me and took my car. My sister must have heard me screaming because Darla came out and tried

141

to chase him down and get him, but he got away. Another black eye. That was my life. Guess what? He was sorry! And I took him back again. He always won me back over with gifts or money. He always knew exactly what I wanted and would use this time to his advantage. Having a hard life and going through the struggle made me tolerate less than I deserved because I didn't even feel like I deserved anything.

In 2014, I lived in a 2-bedroom apartment in Westmont, IL. That was my first apartment in the suburbs. It was small, so Ice was always yelling at the kids and trying to make them stay in their rooms and be quiet. I would always keep Ice's other children. I loved all the kids and took them in like my own. Even when he hated their mom, so he said and didn't want anything to do with the kids, I still took them in because I felt like, as his wife, they were mine too.

I don't remember exactly what we fought about that day. But I vividly recall jumping out of the car and running, and I had two thousand dollars in my pocket.

As I ran, the money fell out of my pocket and flew over the vacant lot I was running in. I stopped and tried to get it, and he caught me. He hit me over and over. He made me pick the money up, and he would knock it back out of my hand. He would constantly fight me and repeat the same steps over and over. He would make me pick the money up and knock it all back out of my hand. Dude was crazy and seemed to be demon-possessed at times. He kept hitting me for so long. I started to scream JESUS! JESUS! JESUS! He stopped swinging and started yelling, "I'mnot scared of that," but he never swung again. Somehow, I was able to call my biological mother, and she came running and ready to fight. She was white and sickly, but she wanted a piece of Ice.

She made it to the city fast, and I don't know how I managed to get away from him that day, but somehow, I got away. She came looking for me and ran into Ice. She had my little sister's dad with her, Carl, and he started fighting Ice, and Ice knocked him out. I started taking my anger out on his money. Every time he fought me, I would race to the house to get his money, so I could plan my exit. I returned to the house, took the money, and went with Carrie. Carrie would show up for this type of stuff once I got older because she acted like she hated Ice. Carrie wanted to take me to her house, but I knew that was the first place he would come looking for me, and he did.

As Carrie and I were at the gas station, we got a call from my little sister crying, saying Ice had run into their house with a knife. He was trying to fight my little sister's dad and Carrie's boyfriend. Carl wacked Ice with a bed rail, and Ice eventually left the house. Ice thought he could go home and sleep after doing all that to me. I had asked my uncle to change the doors' locks so I could go home, but to their surprise, when they arrived, Ice was sleeping in the home. They called the police, and when the police arrived, Ice tried to give them a foot chase. Thanks to Carrie chasing him with the police, they caught him.

I was told he got caught with a gun, and I cried like a baby. Even though I was the victim, I never wanted to see bad things happen to people. I wouldn't say I liked jail and didn't wish it on my worst enemy. I stayed at my cousin's house for the night, and seventeen hundred dollars out of the four six thousand dollars I had taken from the home was missing. Wow! It's unbelievable how people took advantage of me while I was in distress when they were the ones who were supposed to help me. Now I'm guessing you know the rest, right? I didn't press charges, and I was mad at Carrie for trying to press charges because there was no way I could support my lifestyle in the suburbs without him. I didn't want my boys back in the ghetto. My oldest son had started trying to gang-bang, and I was willing to risk my life to save his.

I never really had to deal with cheating, but now he had started beating and cheating on me. I was going through hell. He would love me in the morning and hate me by night. This went on for years, and it just never seemed to get better until the pain changed me. I started selling hair, and my business was booming. It was a time when I bought more money in the house than him. He was intimidated. He wanted to see me do good but never better than him. He wanted me to always need him so that he would always have that control.

I was the first young girl in my city to start selling hair. One of the OG boss ladies put me on. She sold me my first batch of bundles, and I took off. I made bundles and wigs a trend now. I was a trendsetter at this point. I noticed its impact on my city because many other girls started to do it. I was never a hater and always wanted to help or see other girls win. I advised about hair games, and so many young ladies still prosper. He would act like he supported me, but I don't think he ever believed in me. He never trusted me or respected me, so how could this marriage ever work?

Do you know what today is? It's our Anniversary! On 12/31/2015, we were celebrating two years of marriage. We made marriage a trend because everyone felt like if we can do it, they can, too. If we could make it, why not? We had a decorated hotel room and went outside with our mutual friends. Another thing we never agreed on about our friends. He wanted to hang out with the older crowd, and I liked the younger crowd.

He liked to hang around the GDs, and my hood didn't like them, so that was never my favorite thing to do. It was something I refused to do. I was not hanging around the people who were killing the people I grew up with and had love for all my life. I couldn't do it. We celebrated our anniversary by going to dinner, and then we would celebrate our New Year's at night. I found a way to get away from him before the countdown because I never enjoyed being around him with his old drunk-talking friends. I wanted to bring my New Year around the people I had love for. The people I grew up around were fake and haters sometimes, but they were family and the only ones I felt like I had.

The countdown is over, and we're finally into the new year. Ice came to pick me up and beat me to the hotel. He was driving fast and crazy like he was about to kill both of us. He beat me until I had blood coming from everywhere. He stomped my leg so I couldn't run and black my eyes and burst my nose and mouth open. I tried to jump out of the car while it was moving but was unsuccessful. Some good samaritans tried to help me, but he was about to attack and scare them away. He was ruthless.

He pulled up to the pretty hotel decorated to celebrate our anniversary and dragged me into the room. I was helpless at this point. He raped me while bleeding from everywhere. He told me, "Take your clothes off. I want to have sex." I felt hopeless and defeated. I lay there and cried as he humped on my bloody body. It wasn't consensual, but I guess he felt like it wasn't rape because I was his wife. I knew this had to be some of the sickest stuff I had ever been through. Who would want to have sex with somebody after beating them in cold blood like this? It's not right! It's insane.

I knew I was leaving him as soon as I got the opportunity. The next day, we went home, and I didn't say a word. He left to take care of his business, and I left immediately after and went to stay in a hotel. The hate was growing stronger, and all I could think about was killing him. I had to start back smoking weed to calm myself and find another way to deal with this because murder and jail weren't the answer for me. I had children, and I never wanted them to grow up feeling like I did without their mother.

The cycle of abuse is real, and it's scary. I started attending domestic violence groups because I needed some help. I know you are wondering what happened next. If you guessed I went back, you were right because I did. I couldn't find the strength to leave. Besides, where would I go? I had nothing. A few weeks later, I found out I was pregnant with twins. My husband didn't accept something that should have been a blessing to a marriage. It was a bittersweet moment. I was raped, and now I'm pregnant with not one baby but two, and he didn't even want the children. I was devastated. My mama, who raised me, went into the hospital with cancer, and I was stressing heavily. My mama was sick, and I was pregnant, and my intuition was working overtime now that I was back smoking.

Ice came into the house one day, and I had just gotten done smoking. My intuition is like a sixth sense because when I tell you, it tells me to go sit on his lap and go in his left pocket; that's precisely what I did. When I went into his left pocket, that's when I found out he was cheating on me. I pulled a condom out of his pocket and had five different stories about why he had them. Heartbroken again. I went to the hospital the next day and demanded he bring me the call log from T-Mobile, or I would leave. He brought the call log and begged me not to leave. He had been calling his baby mama every day for long periods talking, and here I go, hurt again. He had been lying, cheating, and beating on me all at the same time.

My mother went up for surgery to get the cancer removed, and we believed in God for total restoration. The surgery was risky because she was eighty – six years old, but we trusted in the Lord. I went downstairs to check on the babies, and one of them had passed away. One of my unborn twin's heartbeats was stronger than the other one. One had died while I was two months pregnant. I decided to terminate the whole pregnancy because I was under too much stress, and I knew another baby would only make things worse. I was so hurt when I lost those babies. I always wanted twins.

My mother had defeated stage 2 cancer, and once again, Ice was sorry again. He started taking me on trips and spending more money on me than he had ever spent before. We had never seen that much money while we were together. We went to Mami together and were down there about to fight. He chased me around the whole hotel. We stayed at Fountain Blu; plenty of celebrities were in the building, and I was so embarrassed. I couldn't take him anywhere. He always found something to be mad about; he was a real angry bird. I always liked to dance and sometimes dance wild when I was drinking, but that's something he already knew. He hated that about me, but he wouldn't leave me alone. I liked to turn up. I like to stand on top of couches and tables and get lit and have a ball. That's just what I do!

Mother's Day 2016 was at my house for the family, and I passed out bags filled with money to all the mothers. We had a good turnout, and everything was going well until he got mad and left and took my car. I went out with my friend, and we ran into him outside.

I was playing with him and trying to be funny, and he pushed me so hard that I flew over the curve. I could barely get up, but I limped into my friend's car, and he tried to jump through the window, and I pulled off. He would not let the car go, and I went so fast that he couldn't jump through the window. I turned the music up loud and dragged him six blocks before he finally decided to drop off the car. I was so scared I thought he was dead the way he laid out in the streets. They called me and told me he didn't make it, and I was hysterical because what the hell did I do? Later, I learned it was a lie, and he was okay. I was relieved but scared because I snapped. I also later found out my ACL was completely torn, and I had to get surgery for my right knee because I had no stability in my right knee. My hair business started declining because my mind was just not right.

I dreamed of opening a shop and having my own business, but Ice discouraged me heavily like there was no money in the hair game, and renting a space would not make any money. He would tell me I needed to find a job and stop selling hair. He would speak of fear and doubt about my plans, eventually making me stop believing in myself or anything else.

In 2016, Ice made over three hundred thousand in the streets. He started to really mistreat me that summer. He took his money and left me every weekend. He was cheating on me with a girl from his past and was treating me like I was nothing. He eventually admitted to cheating on me with this girl and took her to the same hotel he had beat me bloody in on our anniversary. Nothing I did was good enough; he talked about me like a dog. He spat in my face and walked all over me. I had the police come out and start getting him arrested, but I never pressed charges. I had been to jail before and didn't think that was the answer.

I was attending church, praying, and believing God would change him, and he did. I didn't know it was going to come to this.

I wouldn't say I liked the way my life was going. I was depressed, and I was lost and constantly losing myself daily. I watched every young girl in the city take off with my dreams and ideas while I never had anyone to believe in me. I started a transportation business, got an LLC for a trucking business, helped him build his credit when I couldn't and encouraged him to get his dealer license. We never went anywhere with any of it because he had no faith in me or anything we were doing. I was losing hope for the future, and the fighting never stopped. I just highlighted in this book the worst situations I experienced that I could remember, but maybe only half the abuse I had to endure. I wanted to stay in a shelter, but I never wanted my kids to go through being homeless and poor. God knew my heart, and I was tired of living like that, so he sent me some help. In 2018, I was called for housing In Ohio. I was so happy! I was scared to go somewhere I had never been and was going alone with my children because Ice couldn't leave his business.

I moved to Ohio on faith, knowing God would lead, guide, and protect me. I didn't have a plan, but God did. I didn't know what would happen next, but knew God was answering my prayers. I worked at McDonald's, three blocks from my house, for the first three months. One day, I watched the news and saw an opportunity to attend Cherry St Mission in Toledo, Ohio, five minutes from my house. They were doing a free call center/ customer service training with help to find a job afterward. I completed the class and met some of the most amazing people there. Indeed, a gift heaven sent. I spoke at the graduation, which was heartfelt with a standing ovation. The crowd was touched. Things were turning around, but I still had one door to close before entering this new chapter of my life.

How could I empower women, give hope, and speak on what I survived while I was still in an abusive situation? I had to end that chapter and heal before walking into new doors. I stayed in Ohio for three months, where I blocked out the world by deleting my social media and started taking my relationship with God and my children to a new level. I stopped smoking weed and started to improve my life. I was living on my own, and I found peace and started to believe in myself that I could live life without my abuser. He caught a case and came down to Ohio to live. He was unhappy. He did nothing to make himself better, and he brought me down while there. He ended up staying six months before abandoning us and breaking my heart again.

As soon as I found the strength to live without him, he came and took his power back and left us again. For years, I had watched him leave us time and time again. It was traumatizing for the children and me. He left for a couple of weeks and popped back up the day following Father's Day a few hours after midnight.

That morning, we woke up, prepared for work and school, and watched him pack his things. My daughter said, "Daddy, can you take me to school today?" He told her, "No! Daddy must take care of some business." It made me so angry, I started telling my daughter to come on because your daddy wants to go with his other kids; he's leaving us. We walked out the door, and I dropped them off at school, went to work, and tried to stay focused. I'm so emotional, and I never knew how to hide what I was going through because I feel everything deeply. I went into the office and tried to act normally, but the tears wouldn't stop. This was the day our marriage changed forever. I had reached my breaking point. I asked them to go home because my uncle died because that's just how hard I was crying. A few hours later, his uncle died, and I was able to secure my job because I knew I had proof. I wasn't grieving the loss of my uncle-in-law; I was grieving the loss of my husband because he walked out on us when I felt like I needed him most. This was one of the highest moments in my life. I was succeeding in the real world, and I thought that was what he wanted, but he didn't

I finally had a higher-paying job and was being offered opportunities to advance and become a manager, but I needed help with my children to work the hours required for the advancement. I was weak to my knees. I went home and just laid on the floor and cried. He was gone again. I hoped he would still be there when I arrived, but I knew he was gone. I cried so poorly all day. Suddenly, a notification went off on my phone, and a young man told me I was gorgeous and he had been looking for me.

I would never say God sent him, but I thank him for sending him, especially at this time. We began to talk, and he was able to take my mind off my circumstances. He was tall, brown, and handsome. He was friendly, respectful, and charming. I enjoyed the conversation and told him I wanted to Facetime him, but I was sick, and he asked me what was wrong. He was a doctor; he could fix it. I melted at the sound of it. I knew he wasn't an actual doctor, but he knew what to say to make me have a better day. Every day for the next two weeks, he became my friend. He called me every morning and checked me after work every night. He became the person I spent my time talking to during my breaks and made me feel so good.

He made me feel seen and acknowledged. I felt special to talk to him. When we Facetime, all we do is smile at each other. It was like a breath of fresh air. Ice had been gone for two weeks and hadn't even called for me or the children once he was gone. The third week had passed by, and it was time for his uncle's funeral, and he had not even told me about it. I used the death of his uncle for the time I needed to get myself together, so I needed to go to the funeral to get the obituary. I was excited to go to Chicago not to see Ice but to talk to my newfound friend. He never wanted me to know his circumstances, so he didn't allow me to see him. He had just come home from jail and beat his case and was under house arrest at his mother's house. He was trying to get back on his feet, and he must not have thought I would accept him for who he was.

I tricked someone into showing me where he lived, and he was so happy to see me. They scared him with what they had to say. They told him Ice would kill both of us if he found out, and he didn't want to fight with another man about his wife, so he started to act differently towards me because I came with problems. Problems he wasn't trying to have.

Ice started chasing me and calling over 100x once he found out I was back in Chicago. Suddenly, he was calling and wanted to be back with me. I wasn't having it. He had left and didn't call and didn't care until he knew I was back in Chicago on the weekends. Now he wanted to talk to me, and that's where things went left for me anyway. My first time back in Chicago, I was jumped on by some of the girls in the neighborhood, and they jumped on one of my friends I brought with me from Ohio, too. I went home, and I started to come back by myself every weekend to Chicago looking for my new friend because I had fallen in love or lust, whatever you want to call it. I loved the way he made me feel. I enjoyed having someone to talk to me and smile while talking.

The following weekend, I was there, and he was mad because I wasn't calling him when I came, but I didn't feel like I had to call him because he wasn't even talking to me at first; now, I was supposed to report him after he left us for dead in a whole different state. Ice was calling like crazy, and I didn't answer the phone. He tried acting like he was in distress and needed my help, but I didn't go. He discovered where I was, popped up, and started fighting me. This was the day I knew it was over forever.

He beat me in front of over one hundred people outside. It was so embarrassing, and only one girl tried to help me and make him stop, but she was unsuccessful. I fought him back like Tina Turner did in the limo with Ike. I fought him back, and it looked like I was winning until he took me off my feet, dragged me by my hair, and hit and kicked me over and over. He was in a rage. He put me in the car, drove down an alley, and choked me until I thought I was going to die. He dragged me out of the car and beat me until he couldn't breathe. He would stop to catch his breath, run up, and beat me some more. He beat me so severely that it was like a little voice came to me and guided me out because I thought I was about to die in that alley. I was bleeding from everywhere. I was covered in my blood. As I could barely breathe, I began to tell him I was sorry and loved him. Like in a scary movie, his head turned towards me and said, "You love me? I said, "Yes, let's go home." He immediately stopped, and we got in the car; he screamed and hit me a couple more times, but we made our way to my mother's house.

I was so happy he was taking me to my mother's house because she lived behind the police station, and I knew I was about to get help. As soon as we pulled up, I jumped out of the car and ran to the police, and they started chasing him. He tried to run into my mother's house, but they caught him and took him to jail. I didn't press charges, but I didn't bond him out of jail or make sure he was okay like all the other times; I went straight home.

A few days later, he showed up on my doorstep, and I was scared. I didn't know what to expect. I could tell I had fought back this time. I wasn't the only one scared. His hair was completely pulled out at the top in the front, his face was scratched up, and his left eye was black. Looking at him really made me feel afraid because I knew he was furious. He didn't look angry at me; instead, he looked sorry. He looked so sorry that I felt terrible for him and was the victim. Once again, I let my heart get the best of me and let him back in again, but the marriage would never be the same.

I ended up pregnant again, and I moved back to Chicago. I knew the love I had for Ice was gone. I stayed there physically, but mentally, I was done. Ice wanted me to have the child so badly, but I knew all it would do was trap me in the marriage. I wasn't about to stay with him; that's all I could think about, so I terminated the pregnancy. I went through enough with him over the last seven years, and I wasn't about to prolong this separation any longer.

I started hanging out with people much younger than me to get closer to my new friend because he was avoiding me at all costs. He wasn't trying to be caught up with another man's wife, which made me want him even more because the next man wouldn't have cared. I argued with Ice night and day and hated how he talked with me. I never wanted to be at home with him, so I stayed in the streets, high and drunk as hell. I lost myself because I started to become the person I once was when I was younger. The pain created a monster again.

Ice was told by one of the younger girls once we got into it with each other that I had a new friend. My new friend was ten years younger than me and didn't have the money Ice had, so that I would help him. She went back and told Ice everything, and Ice became very insecure. Ice started acting crazy. The summer of 2020 got crazy.

Trying to leave Ice put me in an inadequate head space. All I knew was I couldn't live like that anymore, and I would rather die than stay with him, so it felt like I was on a suicide mission trying to leave him because I just knew that it was a possibility I might die behind the things I was about to start doing. I was hanging out with the young guys, ready to give me the guns if needed. My car was in his name at the time, and I was letting little bro Nem drive around in the hood wherever in broad daylight. I just didn't give a fuck no more. Sometimes I was hoping we would get caught outside so they could shoot his ass out of his shoes because, at this point, I hated him. He beat me for years for nothing, and now I was about to give him a reason because I was sick of his shit. I had enough.

Ice started losing his mind. He didn't know what I was doing, and none of the guys ever told him, but he knew I was doing something. I was mistreating him and didn't feel bad about it. He started trying to run my car off the road with his cars. One day, after trying to run me off the road, I returned to the block where he had chased me, and I left the car running with the lights on. The car was tinted so that he couldn't see through it, and I jumped out, sat across the street, and hid in the back of my friend and her husband's car. My friend asked me why I left my car running, and I told her I left it there for bait. "Watch Ice, come do some crazy!" As soon as I told her, Ice came flying up the block and ran straight into a parked car. Everybody couldn't believe he just did some crazy dumb ass shit like that. There were over one hundred people outside. I wasn't even in the car, and Thank God I wasn't!!

I tried to mace Ice, and he let the window up, and the mace bounced back off the window and mace me. I jumped in the car and tried to get away and start driving and passed out from the mace and hit every car on the block. I was scared as hell, and the impact from the hit had woken me up. Scared as hell, I made it three blocks close enough to my mama's house to jump out and run to her for help. They began pouring the milk into my face to help me regain sight. Ice had tried to let the window down to laugh at me, and the mase hit him, too. Bear mace was deadly.

The war between us continued throughout the summer, except he wasn't fighting me anymore. I'd had enough. I maced him before in front of the Cook County Jail and left him there. On another occasion, he had taken my car and phone, and I busted the windows out of his new 40k van. He jumped out of the van while it was moving, trying to snatch me out of the car, and the van was still rolling down the street. Someone on the block had to jump in the van to stop it from crashing into the building while it was moving. Ice didn't even care. All he saw was red, and he was desperately trying to snatch me out of the car but was unsuccessful.

I tried to think of many ways to escape the marriage, but I wanted it to end peacefully. I had thoughts of stealing all his money and disappearing, but then I knew he would chase me for life. I had started messing with another young guy who kept his gun, and when Ice found out about him, he was trying to put money on his head to get him killed. The young dude was ready to smoke Ice, but he said after he killed Ice, he would kill me too, so then I thought to myself that wasn't the way to go. I just wanted it to end peacefully. I didn't care what happened to Ice, but he was still my daughter's father, so I didn't want him to die. In my head, I was always thinking it was either him or me.

One day, it came to me just as clear as day. What did I used to do when I was younger? Why didn't he want to make his wife, then? It came to me that he was a man with pride, and if I started sleeping around, he wouldn't want to be with me anymore because a gangsta in the streets hated to feel like his wife was a hoe. I couldn't get him to walk away when I wanted to, so I had to do something different.

I ended up moving out of the house we lived in together because it just became too toxic for the children to witness, and I knew eventually, one of us would snap. I moved into an apt with my daughter, and my other son was at his grandmother's house while the oldest stayed home with Ice. I started to see this young, fly, scammer guy from out south. Mood was fine. His sex was some of the best sex I ever had. I could only sleep with him twice before things went wrong between us. I would brag to my little cousin and her friends about how good that sex was, and they would all sit around me and listen as if I was a storyteller. A whole week later, my little cousin's friend started to sleep with Mood and told him I was married.

He told me, "He was going to sleep with everything around me," and that's precisely what he did. He slept with my cousin's friends, my friends, and even my stepdaughter; that's when I knew I couldn't deal with him anymore. I was ready to kill the city behind him. The girls from out west were sleeping on him because he was from out south, but I guess I woke them up.

I wasn't sweating them for doing it because they were lying and denying it. Plus, I knew those ladies were scary. My little cousin had this one dirty little friend she grew up with who always messed with the same guys I messed with. I even think she slept with my husband in Miami the night when he and I were fighting because they all disappeared for a while, and nobody even came to check on me, sitting in the lobby all night. She brought her friend out there without telling me she was coming. It was three men I knew she had slept with behind me. The girl had to be secretly obsessed with me and wanted to be me.

I felt like Mood and I had a connection and liked each other, but all that ended. I couldn't blame it all on them. It was my fault he had stopped talking to me. We argued one day, and he didn't call me the next. The day after, I had bet with my little cousin that even though I had not seen Ice, he would still give me whatever I wanted, and I got the van from him and rode the wheels of It and he gave me fifteen hundred dollars.

I was so drunk and was riding so fast and crazy that all my little cousins left me. Why would they leave me drunk driving like that? They couldn't have really cared about me. What if I would have hurt myself? I ended up driving to my mom's house, and Ice was upstairs waiting for me because he knew I would go there on the weekends when I was intoxicated. My boy called me all night and even a couple of times in the morning, but there was no way I could ever answer the phone for him and make it out alive in front of Ice. Mood was gone. He left me. They just fueled the fire by telling him I was married because he didn't know.

As if them backdooring me for my new friend wasn't enough, they told Ice I was seeing him. They told Ice while he was at home with the kids, I would be outside with Mood at least that's what Ice told me they said . My blood cousin Neeski knew how crazy Ice was. She could have gotten me killed telling him something like that, and for that reason, that would be my last time. That was the second or third time she took up for her friend for sleeping with the same man I was around the same time . On top of all that, they were trying to get me killed.

I should have been the one who wanted to fight, but instead, she teamed up with her four fat sisters, a gay friend, and her hoe friend and thought they were going to jump on me in my hood. That would never happen; I shed plenty of blood there, and now I was the Princess of the Mob. No way was my little cousin, whom I had been fighting for all my life, finally get some sisters and think they were going to push on me in my hood over a man I was seeing first. Right after I had busted the Ice windows van windows, I went to get a gun. Thank God I didn't catch him that night . That night went crazy all over the world with everyone in Chicago.

All of 2020, we argued, and he played bumper cars with cars, but he never put his hands on me again because now I had allowed the pain to turn me into a monster. I had learned to live alone in Ohio, and living with him wasn't peaceful. In June 2020, I returned to my oldest son's house, and if you guessed what was next, you were right. I was right back with Ice again. This time, it was because, once again, I felt sorry for him because his mother was fighting COVID-19 and eventually died a few months later. RIP Nosey. She was my girl and knew how it felt to go through what I was going through. She was my girl. I really miss her.

I tried to stay and make it back right, but at this point, it was impossible. I got to the point where I hated him. I hate to see his face mugged up, yelling all the time. I wouldn't say I liked the way he talked to me. The sex was boring now because my heart wasn't in it; all I enjoyed was the head. He knew how fast the police would come in the suburbs, so he was never too aggressive at home, but I became the aggressor. I chased him through the house with butcher knives, and it was like I was the crazy one to the kids now. The kids used to fear Ice, but now they feared me. There had been times when his daughter would see us fighting or arguing and run and get a bat. I felt so bad for the kids because they were traumatized. There were times when they ran out of the house because they were so afraid, and it was time to bring all this to an end.

I got to the point where I would do nothing with Ice in IL. He had to fly me out if he wanted to do dates or quality time because he would never get me to Chicago and do me dirty like usual. The police in the suburbs handled domestic violence way better than the Chicago police. I knew our relationship was ending, so I did what I would call "Ball until I fell." I knew it would be a struggle after I left Ice financially. Every chance I got, I was doing something I always wanted to do to make up for all the days to come that I wouldn't be able to do.

Ice flew me out to Atlanta on New Year's Eve 2020. I always liked going to Florida or Atlanta because they were fun, and I wouldn't say I liked long flights. We spent our last anniversary together. Valentine's Day came, and Ice decorated the house from top to bottom. Rose petals and roses from the stairs to all around the room. Candles were lit everywhere. Balloons and bouquets of roses covered my bedroom. I had groomed him to be a wonderful man, but I knew he would never be the man I groomed him to be with me. I knew he needed someone else to be the best version of himself because he got used to treating me the way he treated me. I taught Ice many things, especially how to treat a woman; unfortunately, I would never get the love I desired from him. The man I knew he had become would never be at his best with me. I taught Ice to be romantic, buy roses, and decorate rooms. Unfortunately, I made him a better man for the next woman because even though he had finally changed, I also changed, but I changed for the worse. I poured into him and built him from the ground up while he tore me down and broke me into pieces. I had lost my identity, and I could no longer be the good wife I once was anymore, sadly. I was utterly broken. My heart was cold.

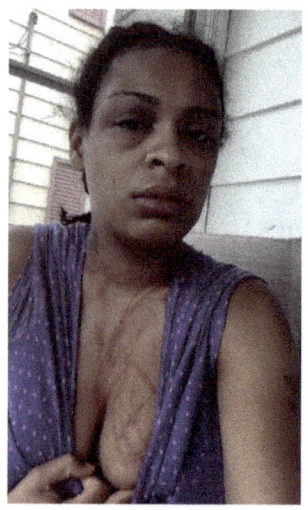
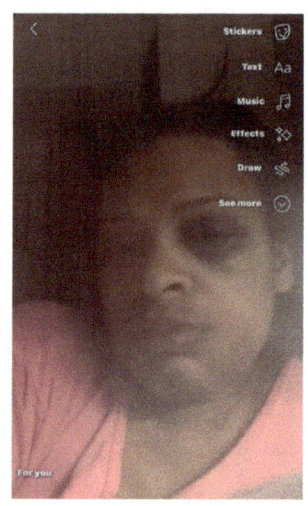

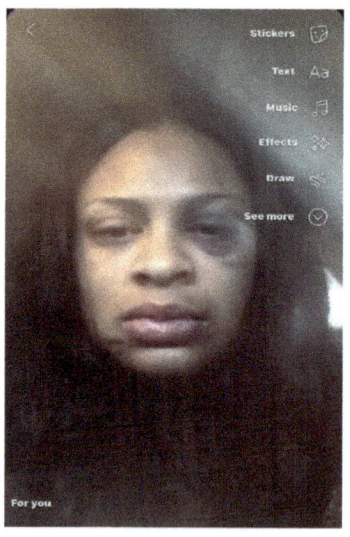

Chapter 10: Be Free

Whom the Son Sets Free is Free Indeed – John 8:36

Back to raq! Well I didn't live directly in Chicago but that is where I went when I left home for fun. 45 mins away from Chicago February 15, 2021, I was invited to attend a What's Love seminar on Zoom. I listened to the speakers and heard them say if he had abused me before, he would do it again. I had heard all this before, but today, it hit differently. I spoke about my situation because I had never been scared or too prideful to tell my story, and a lady offered me her life coaching classes for free. It was much needed and appreciated. Ice had been gone since 6 am that day, and I was home alone all day, and the kids were gone. We had been going through a few episodes over the last month where he couldn't let go of what my little cousins told him about Mood. Even though he was not talking to me anymore, Ice didn't know that and was determined to find out what was happening. I guess he looked at him as a threat, and I know why because he saw his younger self in him.

Ice made it home that night around 10 pm, and I was asleep. He came in angry and woke me from my sleep, going crazy. He was screaming, "You're still talking to that nigga. I'm like, "what are you talking about?" Ice had been stalking the boy on social media, and earlier that day, he posted the first three digits of his phone number, letting people know he had lost his other phone and asking them to call that number. Ice went through the entire call log, found the man's number, and called him. I was so embarrassed and angry because why was he doing all this? Did he decorate a beautiful room yesterday to start a fight today? I was fed up! That man wanted nothing to do with me, and Ice was driving me crazy about him. I had gone to Mood's birthday party a week before, but we didn't even say two words to each other. When I got home, Ice had ripped my Louie Purse off me, and I had to call the police to get him escorted out. The day of my son's birthday party, a few days before Valentine's Day, he wanted to argue with me about it and messed up the whole party.

I couldn't take any more. He was screaming; he called Mood, and I asked him what he said. He said, "he told me to quit playing with him." I told Ice to "GET OUT!!" Now, I was screaming and going crazy because I was fed up. After all the stuff he had done to me, did he think I was gone be sorry that I finally started doing shit? I wasn't sorry, and I wasn't scared!! I was tired, and I would rather die than keep going through the abuse. I know it sounded selfish, but I couldn't do it anymore. I was dying slowly inside, and it was safe to say I had lost my mind.

Ice tried for months to get me back, but I didn't let up this time. I would still call him for sex and money because, after being in a long-term relationship, my body didn't understand what was going on. When I would get drunk, my body would crave his sex. I knew I could always call him if I couldn't get the man I wanted. I had a person I was attracted to sexually, but we knew it would never work between us. He would play games with me and have sex with me whenever he wanted to. He wouldn't come when I wanted him, but he would call when he wanted it.

A month later, after I put Ice out, he went out of town, and I knew he was with a girl, but honestly, I didn't care. He left ten thousand dollars at my house and all his clothes. I begged him to get all his stuff, but he didn't. When he returned from out of town, he told me to bring his things and money and drop them off at his sister's house. No way in hell was I about to do that. I didn't tell him to leave this here. When he finally decided to get his things, I bleached everything and tried to bleach him too. I kept the ten thousand and told him bye. He left and knew never to return. I had lost my mind, and he knew it.

April 2021 was my birthday month, and nobody had ever thrown me a party. And I had some money now, so I planned the biggest birthday party ever and had the most fun birthday ever. I only had maybe five girls there, but all the guys showed up, showed me love, and gave me gifts. I love my brothers. They were not my real family, but it was the only family I ever felt like I had in the streets. They showed up for me in ways my real family never did. They wouldn't let anybody hurt me; when times were hard, they were there. They had fake ways when it came to bro code, but in most cases, I had earned my stripes and was one of them.

In May 2021, I saw all my bros in Miami living life. These were the same brothers I started with; now, we all had little money. We were from 2800 Hollywood and knew how to make a little look like a lot. Even when we didn't have anything, we made it happen and made the struggle look good. My boys were in fast cars at the biggest house, and I hopped on a flight out of the blue and got down there by myself. The whole hood was there when we had the time of our life. On my first night there, I was so drunk and having so much fun, I lost my wallet or maybe somebody stole it, but it had three thousand hundred-dollar bills in there with my credit cards and ID. I woke up hysterical.

God always seems to shine his light on me in dark places. At first, I was going crazy and sad. Then it came to me to relax. I wore my swimming suit and went to the rooftop pool for a swim. As I calmed down, I thought about how my cards were connected to my cash app on my phone and how I still had three thousand more on a card. Won't he do it!! One of the demons from the 2800 gave me cash when I cashed her the money. The show must go on! I felt fine that night and went outside. Some brothers were on the strip, and I hopped in the car with them. We went to the mansion where everybody else was.

They were out shooting videos because some of them were rappers. I knew my hood knew some of the hottest rappers in the game. Out of the crew, it was one

I knew I wanted. To my surprise, he came walking through the door. I could not believe my eyes. The one I wanted was standing right here in front of me. I didn't want to seem thirsty, so I said nothing to him. I didn't know him, nor did I know anything about him; I just felt like he was the one. I didn't even know his name and had never heard about him. I just had seen him on the videos and knew he was the one. We were all getting in cars and about to leave. He asked one of the brothers for a square. Bro didn't smoke, but I was standing right there, and I did. Bro told me to give him a square, and I was delighted, too. I asked him if it was anything else, he wanted out my purse in a funny way, and he asked for my number.

We went out and partied, and we had a good time. I acted a fool as usual. I had been going through so much in my life that I would just get so intoxicated to the point I was an entirely different, wild, crazy person. The next day, I woke up and saw I had missed a call. I called the number back and to my surprise it was him- The Hero! He told me to come see him, and I got in an Uber and went straight to him. He was on the fiftieth floor in one of Miami's nicest, richest-looking buildings. It was love at first sight. The view was amazing, and he was sexy as hell to me. His body looked like it was made of steel. I noticed one of his hands wouldn't open, but it didn't matter. I finally got him. We had the best sex that day. I was so attached to him. His energy was everything. He made me feel warm and safe in his presence. I connected with him instantly.

Later that day, he called for me, but I had gone outside with the girls. I was on cloud nine, but I missed my beat with him that night. The next day, I flew back home. I thought somebody may have told him bad things about me because I didn't have the best reputation and was the most hated in the city. He finally responded and asked me to get him from the airport. He asked me for fifteen hundred dollars, and he would give it back, and I gave it to him. Money wasn't was a thing to me then, so I thought nothing of it. The hero made me feel so good. We talked, rode around the city, and people saw us together, and I knew the hate would start.

The last thing people wanted to see was me make it out the streets with a rapper or any man for that reason.

I would be lying if I denied that I wasn't living right. I wasn't in my right state of mind, and I became very toxic and heartless. I was lost and broken. I was hurt and confused. I had no goals, no desire to change, and all I did was get high and drunk and party to avoid the pain. I felt hopeless. I knew eventually I would go broke, so I lived every moment like it was my last. I wasn't completely free from marriage just yet. I didn't even really know if I would make it out alive. I just lived for today and will forget tomorrow until I was introduced to my hero...

He asked me why my name was out here so bad, and all I could tell him was about the things I had to endure over the years. He gave me a chance, and he was patient with me. I loved him on sight, but now I was about to find out why. He stood for something, and he was strong. He was handsome and humble. He was determined, goal-driven, and loyal to the ones he loved. He loved his family and his children and would die for his brothers. I loved what he valued, and his confidence turned me on. He had been through a lot, and life wasn't easy for him. He spent ten years in jail and gave the rest of the time he was sentenced back. He had been shot over twenty times in his home. His grandma raised him. Granny had a scar on her face, just like mine, and she was a sweet and brilliant lady. It seemed like he could see right through me. He understood me in ways I didn't even understand myself.

He spoke life into me and encouraged me to find ways to flip my money. He told me I was Queen and wasn't like these other girls. He didn't understand why I acted the way I did because he saw me as unique, and he knew I had something in me that was bigger than how I acted. He saw things in me that I didn't even see in myself. He believed in me when I lost all hope. He encouraged and inspired me to love myself. I loved him because of how he loved and adored me. I learned so much about myself and how toxic I had become after going through so much in previous relationships. I didn't know how to love, and I was set in my toxic ways, and I didn't even know it.

The way he moved was different, and I didn't understand him, nor did I trust him. I didn't even trust myself. After building me up all the time, I felt better about myself, and once I started dealing with him, I never had sex with Ice again, and I ultimately ended the relationship with Ice. I divorced Ice. That's why I named him the "Hero!" He saved me from a toxic marriage and self-destruction. He said it was his job as a man to build me up and make me feel better about myself. He was different from any man I ever dealt with in my whole life. He was stable and in control of his emotions. He was a gangster and a gentleman. He was a very hardworking and powerful man. I loved him so much!

After encouraging me to learn ways to turn 4,000 into 40,000, I joined a team that taught us how to trade in the foreign exchange market. I learned so much from them. I fell in love with the process of healing. I had a life coach with whom I worked on boundaries and healing, but when I joined this team, they made us focus on mindset. The mindset was one of the most important lessons I learned during my healing process.

God spoke to me one day and told me I would have to allow Ice to be happy with another woman and be at peace while it happens to leave peacefully. A few weeks later, after not having sex with Ice for over a month since I met The Hero, Ice started posting on social media that he had a new woman. He came outside with her and flaunted his new woman in my face in front of everyone, and I did not care. I was so in love with the Hero and what he stood for, I would never want to look Ice away again. I had no hard feelings towards Ice, but it was over for good!

I was free at last and very happy about it. The sad part of it was now I was broken and toxic and not mentally stable. I was not ready to be in a relationship, and I started to hurt the one God sent in my life to help me heal. I was investing in The Hero, and I would do whatever he asked me for. I started to feel used because I didn't understand his way of moving. I was disrespectful and very mean at times when I was mad.

I would love him today and hate him tomorrow, which was part of a cycle of abuse I endured for years. It was hard for him to take me seriously because I said I loved him in the morning and was ready to leave by night.

I had reasons to feel how I felt and be guarded the way I was. I was vulnerable, and I had zero tolerance for bullshit. I didn't understand what he meant by taking things slow. I felt like I was being manipulated and played. The hero was a very good person but had toxic traits himself. He was a liar and a cheater. He was also emotionally unavailable. I have never been in a healthy relationship, and I didn't understand anything about dating after being in such a toxic marriage. I highly recommend taking the time to heal before dating. I wish I had known then what I know now. I wasn't ready for what he was trying to do with me, and I ended up hurting him in the end, but I thank God every day for him because I don't know where I would be without him. Even though it was terrible to date while being broken, had I not dated, I never would have even realized all the toxic things I inherited from the abuse.

Winter 2021 – the healing begins. I had to start with my mindset first. All these years, I was told I was a hoe, I was nothing, I wasn't worthy, I would never be anything, I was crazy, and I was just a hood chick who lost out on her chance to become anything in life. After being beaten the way I was for over twenty years off and on, I didn't feel like I was anything. I was bright and pretty, but I felt less than trash inside. I didn't even think I deserved to be loved. I even felt like I didn't deserve a good man. I lost all hope.

I wrote this book because I want you all to know there's hope. I was hopeless, and I stopped believing in myself, and I had no dreams or goals. By the grace of God and through prayer, I was lost, but now I'm found. As I attended the meetings with the Run the Play Family and listened to Mornings with Neno, they helped me renew my mindset. I had to learn to reprogram my mind. I had to start to see myself as the person I wanted to become, and I had to speak those things that weren't as though they were. I started working on speaking positive affirmations day and night and developing a positive morning routine.

Developing positive habits and trying to drop toxic habits was hard. I had no dreams or goals when I started doing visualization meditations. I just visualized myself waking up sober and being grateful daily for what I have now. I had to see myself waking up happy, praying, being thankful, and reading God's word every day, even if it's only one scripture. After three to four months of visualizing myself just waking up, praying daily, being sober, and being grateful for my manifestations, which have come to life for over a year, I've successfully developed healthy morning routines. I mastered waking up early, praying, and being grateful after constantly waking up mad and arguing for years; I'm finally at peace. No matter what my circumstances are right now, I'm grateful. I pray, am thankful, and put God's word in me daily to renew my strength. The word is like life to the body and soul. It feeds, nourishes, and strengthens my soul. I believe the key to a better life is learning to be grateful for where you are right now. You'll learn to attract more things to be grateful for.

After four months of visualizing myself developing a morning routine, I finally have a dream and vision for myself and what I want to accomplish. I visualize myself writing this book and becoming a transformational speaker and life coach. If you're reading this right now, another one of my manifestations has come to life. If you can see it, you can be it! All you must do is believe it! I know it sounds super easy, right? But believing is the hardest thing to do when your bank account is negative and you don't see the light. I'm here to tell you that if I could do it, you can too. Never give up on your dreams. Life is hard, and you go through different tests and trials, but it will get better if you hold on and put in the work. The meantime in-between time is what tests your faith. It could look like you are never going to make it. You must believe in yourself. Even if you don't believe in yourself, believe in God. I wouldn't have made it this far without him. I had to have something bigger than myself to believe in because I never could have made it in my strength. It all starts in your mind. Forgive yourself, look forward, and don't look back. It's neither easy nor comfortable, but the uncomfortable situation is where growth begins.

I'm focusing on healing after the trauma. Self-mastery and discipline. I educated myself on everything I wanted to change or improve by watching YouTube videos and reading self-help books. I wanted to increase my knowledge by watching mentors and listening to audio about building my business credit and the habits of millionaires. I slowed down on the parting, started to lock in, and got serious about my goals. It took me almost two years to write this book, but I finished it. I started taking my health seriously and began exercising and stretching yoga. I still struggle with healthy eating but am still growing and learning daily. I don't think I have become the best version of myself, but I'm growing and developing new ways to live daily.

Learning to love myself for who I was despite my mistakes. I'm not my mistakes! It was easy to forgive everybody but myself. Taking the time to learn and develop new ways to live. Learning to forgive and be patient with myself was hard. Nobody talks about how the healing may hurt more than the wounds, but trouble doesn't always last, and this, too, shall pass. Life is hard. Healing is hard. Being broken is harder. It takes time to heal. Nothing happens overnight. Just start to make small changes daily over a long period, and you will see a massive breakthrough in due season. It's called the compound effect. Put the work in and be consistent. Get in your bag and out your feelings, and take your crown back. Trust the process. You have the power to change your future. Don't sleep on yourself. You will have trouble in this world, but be at peace because Jesus has already overcome the world. Forget the things that are behind you and focus on what lies ahead.

So, if you are reading this right now, it's safe to say

I MADE IT!!

More to come!! You can make it too! Just hold on! I had suicidal thoughts, moments of weakness, moments of regrets, and moments of unbelief, and you will, too. I had times when I didn't think I would make it, and I just wanted to give up. But that's where your God will strengthen your weakness and give you the power to push through. Take all your problems to God in prayer. You can't make in your strength, but with God, nothing is impossible. I'm a living witness. Use the word to clean you from the inside out. It may not seem like it's doing anything but just read one scripture daily. The word will renew your mind and transform your trauma into triumph. I started just reading one Psalms a day. David was a worshiper. It would help if you praised your way out even when you don't feel like you have the victory yet. I'm not yet where I want to be, but I'm not who I was. I thank God for how far I have come.

I wrote this book. I'm taking life coaching classes and preparing myself to be a keynote speaker. I'm the best mother I could be right now, striving to improve. By God's grace, my oldest son Pimpfunta went to college on a D1 scholarship for football. It's turning around for me. I'm still a work in progress because even though I don't hang out in the streets anymore, I still like to party and turn up, but God isn't finished with me yet. I'm still a work in progress, and I believe I'llimprove. Being great takes time, and I have come a long way, and I know I still have a long way to go.

Stay Tuned – The healed version of me is coming soon.

YOU ARE AMAZING!!

YOU ARE STRONG!!

YOU ARE IMPORTANT !!

Your life matters!!

Believe IN Yourself !!

I believe in you !!

YOU CAN DO IT!!

YOU ARE LOVED!!

YOU ARE WORTHY !!

YOU ARE VALUABLE !!

KEEP GOING !!!

YOU GOT THIS !!!

I LOVE YOU!!

GOD LOVES YOU!!!

When God is for you, it's more than the world against you!!

God is within you!!

YOU CAN'T FAIL!!

FAILURE IS ONLY REDIRECTION!!!

HEAD UP KINGS & QUEENS!!

BETTER DAYS ARE AHEAD!!!

All things new Loading.......

Healing To be continued ….

Stay Tuned ……

IT AINT OVER!!

Author Information

Hello, I'm Charity the author of A Gift Of A Curse, a powerful memoir that tells the true story about my life. I was raised on the west side of Chicago by my adoptive parents after my birth mother gave me away due to racism and generational curses. My life has been filled with unbelievable turn of events that will make you laugh and cry, as I share my heartfelt story of pain and heartbreak.

Growing up, I had to survive gangs, bullying, addiction, abuse, and domestic violence. I never gave up hope. I wanted to share my story in a way that would inspire young people to never choose the same path that I did, and to give hope to those who feel like their situation will never get better.

My purpose for writing this book is to encourage someone to choose life and to inspire readers to believe in themselves again. I want to speak life into my readers and allow my pain to give them power. Encouraging readers to never give up on their dreams. Speak and think positive and you well attract more positive outcomes.

Contact me at: charitydun.org

Website: www.charitydun.com

Instagram: Iamcharitydun

Facebook: Charity Dun